# Art Infusion

## K–5 Art Activities to Enrich...
## Social Studies, Science, Math, Language Arts

by Susie Kropa
Illustrated by Susie Kropa

Cover Design by Susie Kropa and Seth Schaller


ISBN: 1-56490-207-2
Printing Number: 9 8 7 6 5 4 3 2 1

Gary Grimm & Associates
P.O. Box 378
Carthage, IL 62321
www.ggapublishing.com

I would like to acknowledge the dedication of classroom teachers everywhere—
and especially those I worked with in Mt. Pleasant, Iowa.

# Table of Contents



 

## Fun With Art

## PREFACE

The arts matter! As an elementary art teacher, I have observed and worked closely with many classroom teachers and thousands of children. Some teachers understand how the arts enrich the everyday curriculum and motivate students to learn. But for the most part what elementary teachers call "art" is truly busywork. Art is a discipline that can be taught and learned. The classroom teacher has the advantage of helping students understand that art is the common thread that runs through all areas of life and study. I wrote this book to encourage you to think about art not as just a period of time set apart each week for making stuff, but as an important part of your curriculum.

Research has shown that our brains are not programmed *just* to learn facts. The two sides of the brain give us the mind and spirit that make us human. The left side is dedicated to the accumulation of factual knowledge, which is often defined as the "basic skills." The right side manages insight. It gives us "AHA!" moments. It is intuitive and illogical. The right side is in control when we are moved to tears over the beauty of a symphony or a magnificent view, when we dance for joy, when we draw or paint what we cannot speak, when we reveal inner thoughts in poetry and song. The arts—the "human"ities—make us fully human.

Why is visual art so often misused in the elementary classroom? First, elementary teachers have a full plate, including: overwhelming responsibilities in dealing with the expectations of parents, school administrators, and legislators; managing children with horrendous, chaotic home lives on one hand, and children with over-indulgent parents, on the other; conferencing with children and parents of many nationalities who haven't yet mastered English. Secondly, you may not have had an art class since elementary school and wouldn't know where to begin. Consequently, "art" becomes mindless, entertaining, assembly-line sorts of seat work that mainly mean following directions. Skills may indeed be learned from manipulating the materials, but there is little emotional involvement. A "GOOD JOB!" is "coloring inside the lines" or not using too much glue.

All students, regardless of social standing, nationality, or IQ, need an outlet for self-expression. Art is part of life. It goes hand in hand with the so-called basic skills. Rather than setting it apart, art can make everything you teach richer. Teaching art is like coaching. As you practice together, you and your students will develop mental and physical skills, learn to deal with failures and frustrations, and experience the great feelings of accomplishment that come with perseverance. I hope this book will encourage you to start thinking about art in a new way. You will find a variety of motivational techniques, suggestions for an aesthetic classroom learning environment, and lessons that you can use year after year. You will discover the art of teaching art!

 

# THE CLASSROOM—YOUR HOME AWAY FROM HOME

We get so used to the rooms we inhabit that we no longer see them with a critical eye. Invite a friend or colleague to look at your classroom at different times during the year. Ask for an honest assessment of the learning environment.

## CREATING A HEALTHY ATMOSPHERE FOR LEARNING

1) Model good housekeeping. This is a valuable lesson not found in the curriculum. Messes are inevitable at times, but I've been in classrooms where there was no room to breathe! With guidance, students can learn where to find things in the room and should be expected to return books and supplies to their proper places.

2) What kinds of visuals do you use? And how many? With so many choices available, it's easy to go overboard with color and excess. Imagine your own living room with different-colored shades on the windows, walls painted in broad stripes of bright colors, cartoony pictures on the walls, and 25 colorful objects dangling from the ceiling. Too often this is the decorative approach to the elementary classroom. It's the visual equivalent of noise. Children encounter it almost everywhere they go. Is it any wonder there are so many attention deficit problems? Critically assess your classroom's visual comfort level.

### SUGGESTIONS

1) Use one color on all (or most) of the bulletin boards, a color you can live with all year. Neutral or pastel colors make good backgrounds for almost anything you want to display. (There are exceptions, as in the suggestion on page 104.)

2) Instead of cartoon characters or commercial images, use a few reproductions—fine art or children's book illustrations. The *Art Image Publications* catalog has a nice selection of reproductions at a reasonable price. *Crizmac, Art and Cultural Education Materials, Inc.* offers a wealth of multicultural materials, including reproductions, posters, and original artwork you could use to decorate your classroom. If your budget is really tight, there are calendars that feature the art of individual artists or arts of different cultures. Don't forget rummage sales, where you'll often find interesting sculptures, toys, and still-life materials at little expense. In addition to exposing children to great art, the pictures and artifacts can provide inspiration for writing assignments, drama, and music, as well as art projects.

3) Photographs—as a thank-you gift, charitable organizations often send calendars with beautiful wildlife, floral, and landscape photography. Good visuals motivate children to observe and include more details in their drawings. While the ideal experience is firsthand observation, photographs will work. You will find tips about drawing from photographs on pages 16, 19, and 20.

# Growth and Development in Art

Art educator Viktor Lowenfeld, in his book *Creative and Mental Growth*, describes the stages children typically go through in their artistic development. The first stage (18–24 months) is scribbling, the precursor of drawing and writing. Scribbles gradually progress from random to more deliberate marks, including circles. At the age of three or four, children begin drawing rudimentary people; at first, just a face with arms and legs attached, then head, body, and limbs. By the time they start kindergarten, most children are drawing people and other things that interest them. Children are asked to draw a person to help predict their readiness for school.

**Schematic Stage:** *Schema* means a symbol for something real. At about age five or six, children develop their own schema for everything they draw. The schema gives them a sense of security.

**Human Schema** refers to the symbols used for hands, feet, faces, and other features that may describe the human figure. Taken out of context, the symbols may not have meaning, like a triangle for a nose. Notice the wide variety in the schema below.

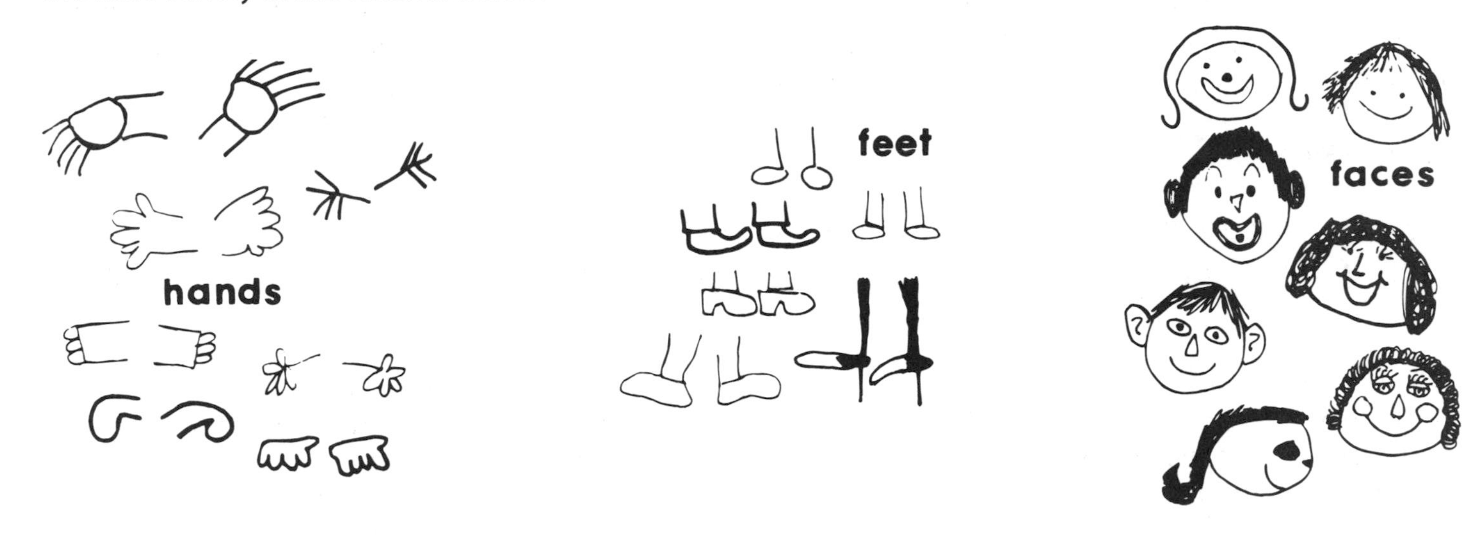


**Space Schema** is the organization of objects on a line rather than floating all over the paper, as is typical of preschool drawings. Lowenfeld calls it the "baseline."
*Bent Baseline*: Children at this level are so tied to the baseline that they will do interesting things to preserve it. For instance, drawing a hill or mountain requires a bent or curved rather than straight line. This is still a baseline, in that everything on the line is perpendicular to it! If you could straighten out the line by pulling on it, everything would be "correct" and on a baseline. You can see the same thing on the rooftops of houses. Notice how the chimneys lean over. Bent baseline!

*Fold-overs*: Drawing both sides of a street or river presents a problem which children may solve by drawing half of the scene upside-down. If you fold the paper up on either side of the street, the picture makes sense. Drawing a table presents the same problem. In this case, if the legs are folded down, it reads correctly. Sometimes the baseline is left out altogether, as in a picture of people sitting around a blanket having a picnic or in any depiction of a sporting event. It is not uncommon to see several views in one picture in an attempt by the artist to show everything.

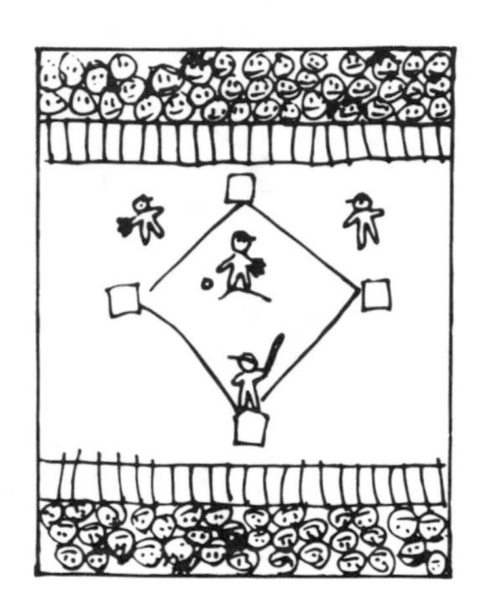

**Other Characteristics of the Schematic Stage:** Sometimes children will draw X-ray pictures, showing both the inside and the outside of a building or below the surface of the ground, as seen in the examples.

**Color:** The use of color has changed from the preschool anything goes to a rigid perception of the "correct color." The sky is blue, grass is green, and the sun is yellow. Color usage may not be the same for every child. For instance some children use orange or red for the sun. Whatever their choice, once a color is assigned, it is used repeatedly. Motivation can alter their perception—fields in the fall, sunset skies, or stormy weather, for example.

**Design:** At this stage children are intuitively good designers. Repetition of the schema creates a natural rhythm in their pictures. They also have a sense of composition, organizing the picture in an interesting way.

**Variations in the Schema:** Children can be encouraged to go beyond their "safe" schema through motivation. The examples below show how the schema for trees has been altered. First graders were asked to draw a tree on one half of the paper. Then they went outside and, gathering around a tree, not only observed the different colors they saw in the leaves, but also felt the roughness of the bark and *became* a tree by stretching their arms up and spreading their fingers, trying to imagine leaves growing from their fingertips. They drew a second tree on the other half of the paper. Who can argue with motivation?

**The Gang Age:** Lowenfeld called the intermediate grades the Gang Age long before "gang" had a negative image. He was referring to the feeling of camaraderie among peers of this age, when they begin to separate themselves from their parents and other adults. Their friends become more and more important. Cliques form. Friendships and interests tend to separate by sexes. The wishes of the group influence the individuals in it. ("EVERYBODY has a cell phone, Mom!") The evolution from egocentric beings to social beings brings about changes in the way they perceive and characterize their world.

**The Figure:** Older children reject the generalizations of the schema. They perceive and want to draw more details to make things look "real." Figures show definite male/female characteristics in faces, hair, and clothing. What is gained in attention to detail is lost in the spontaneity which makes younger children's art so charming. Gang Age drawings look stiff in comparison. Lowenfeld makes a distinction between "realism" and "naturalism." Gang Agers draw "realistically" in the sense that their drawings describe what is real to them.They do not draw according to the laws of nature. For instance, although an article of clothing may be pictured with the correct number of buttons, the natural folds of the fabric will be left out. See page 50.

**Color, Space, and Design:** Gang Age use of color is broader than it was at the Schematic Stage. Children are aware of tints and shades and are willing to experiment with expressive uses of color to create mood.

The baseline is replaced with a new understanding of space. By third grade children are beginning to understand the illusion of depth or the "plane." They will show near and far by drawing several layers of ground and will attempt to draw front/side views of buildings. Sometimes roof lines present perspective problems they can't quite figure out—but they try! For some reason, the sun often appears in the upper left or right corner of the sky. The sky not only meets the ground, but also may have colors that indicate the weather, season, or time of day.

Gang Agers are conscious designers as compared to the intuitive nature of design at the Schematic Stage. They are ready to think about "composition," the ordering of the elements in a picture, and they are able to create complex symmetric and radially symmetric designs.

# Drawing

Throughout the elementary years, and especially in the primary grades, students are asked to draw. Most kindergartners are eager to comply, but as children move through the grades, many become less secure in their drawing ability. In the core courses, students start with the basics and gradually learn, in a variety of ways, to deal with complexity. Likewise, their drawings gradually move from simple shapes and symbols to more naturalistic representations of the world. This is not to say that fifth graders draw *better* than kindergartners. They just draw differently. Did you know that most adults' drawing development stops at about the fifth-grade level? Fifth grade is the end of art instruction in many school systems. If you have no art teacher to help you, this book should give you ideas about handling the "how do you draw (fill in the blank)" questions, drawing expectations for different grade levels, and techniques and tricks to help your students draw with confidence. Drawing is neither busy work nor a waste of time. It's another way of knowing.

Many of the projects in this book start with drawings. If you can do **only** the drawing and not the rest, do the drawing.

**Sketchbooks**

At the beginning of the school year, make a sketchbook for every child in your class plus a few extras. Staple together 10–15 sheets of white copier paper for each book plus 2 colored sheets for front and back covers. Your first art lesson can be to have the students decorate the covers of their sketchbooks. If you don't want the books sneaking out at the wrong times, store them in a filing cabinet or on a shelf for easy access. Issue new ones as needed.

# Still Life

"Still life" refers to arrangements of objects on a table and to *pictures* of these arrangements. An artistic eye is involved in both setting up a still life and drawing it. Traditional still lifes might include different kinds of dishes, varieties of foods, or vases of flowers in front of a drapery of some kind. A still life arrangement can be an ever-changing part of your classroom decor, with creative and visually inspiring **themes** that could relate to science, social studies, nutrition, the seasons, sports, hobbies—think creatively! A still life arrangement can fill a whole table or a tiny spot in a corner. If you don't have much room, you can compose a still life in a cardboard box. Cut off one end and one side of the box, drape a piece of cloth over it, then add whatever objects you want to use.

In terms of composition, a still life arrangement should have objects of different sizes. Also it's a good idea to use props (books would work) underneath the drapery so that the objects are on different levels, rather than all lined up in a row. In fourth and fifth grade, if you begin the year setting up still lifes yourself, at some point you could appoint a couple of interested students to be the Still Life Committee.*

*Disclaimer—as an art specialist I haven't tried this committee idea myself, but I *have* had students who enjoyed doing that sort of thing and could handle it.

# *Mixed Media and More*

As a classroom teacher you probably want to keep your art projects fairly simple and stress-free. Pencil drawings would be the least messy. However, some projects which start out as pencil drawings beg for more. Here are some ways to take the pencil drawing further.

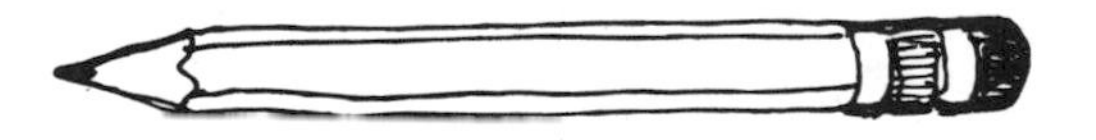

**PENCIL PLUS**

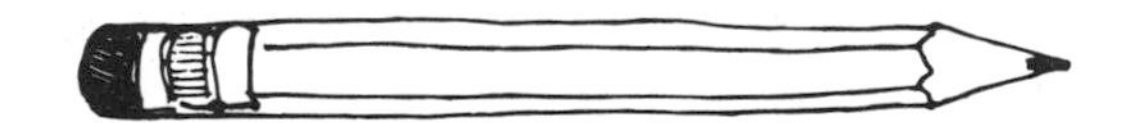

**Black Sharpie permanent marker:** line drawings retraced with black Sharpie permanent marker are bolder and easier to see at a distance. (If a drawing includes a lot of pencil *shading* it's better left as is.) Also, using the black Sharpie permanent marker is a good step before any kind of **color** is added

**Color:** typical choices would be **crayons, colored pencils, markers,** or **watercolors**, all fairly easy to do in the classroom, either as a whole group or center activity. The question is when to use which medium or combination of media. One of my favorite techniques is crayon resist. Students color parts of their pictures pretty heavily with crayon, then fill in large areas with **wet watercolor.** Students will dip hands in clean water and lightly wet the paper all over, then use a soft, wet brush to paint color(s) in the empty spaces. This works well for painting all kinds of skies (p. 14). Be sure to experiment yourself before you try anything new with your class. It's a good idea to demonstrate the process, including how to correct mistakes (which in the case of wet watercolors may mean quickly blotting the boo-boo with a paper towel).

**PAINTS and BRUSHES**

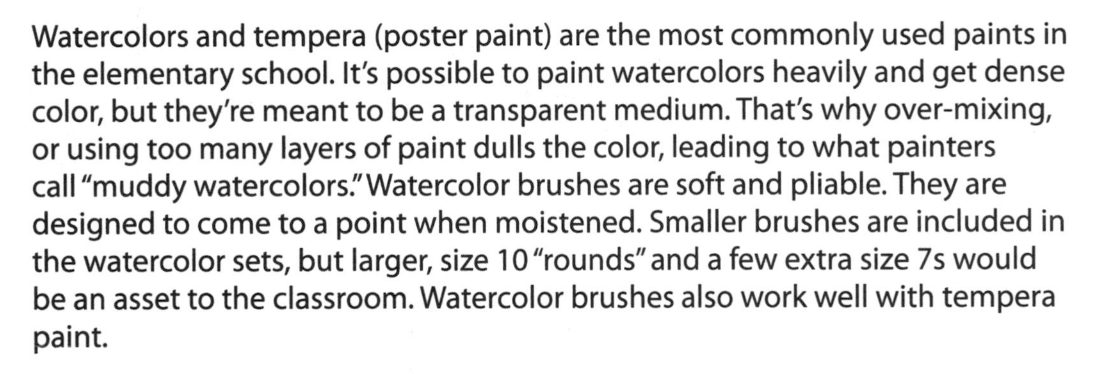

Watercolors and tempera (poster paint) are the most commonly used paints in the elementary school. It's possible to paint watercolors heavily and get dense color, but they're meant to be a transparent medium. That's why over-mixing, or using too many layers of paint dulls the color, leading to what painters call "muddy watercolors." Watercolor brushes are soft and pliable. They are designed to come to a point when moistened. Smaller brushes are included in the watercolor sets, but larger, size 10 "rounds" and a few extra size 7s would be an asset to the classroom. Watercolor brushes also work well with tempera paint.

Tempera paints are opaque. One color will completely cover another, provided the first color is dry. If not, the two colors will mix to make a new color. Both techniques are valuable and children will learn them with practice. Tempera bristle brushes are coarser and blunt. I would recommend ½" and ¼". Classroom brush sets are available, but I've found that just the combination of watercolor and tempera brushes I've named is enough.

It's important to wash brushes thoroughly after use, and always store them "hair in the air." Some kids love to wash all the brushes after a painting session!

 

# Paper Techniques

**Five-point Star**— Every February my friend Phyllis taught her second-graders this trick, and they made a huge wall-sized flag, with all the students contributing a star or two. Begin with a square of white or colored copier paper, fold and cut.

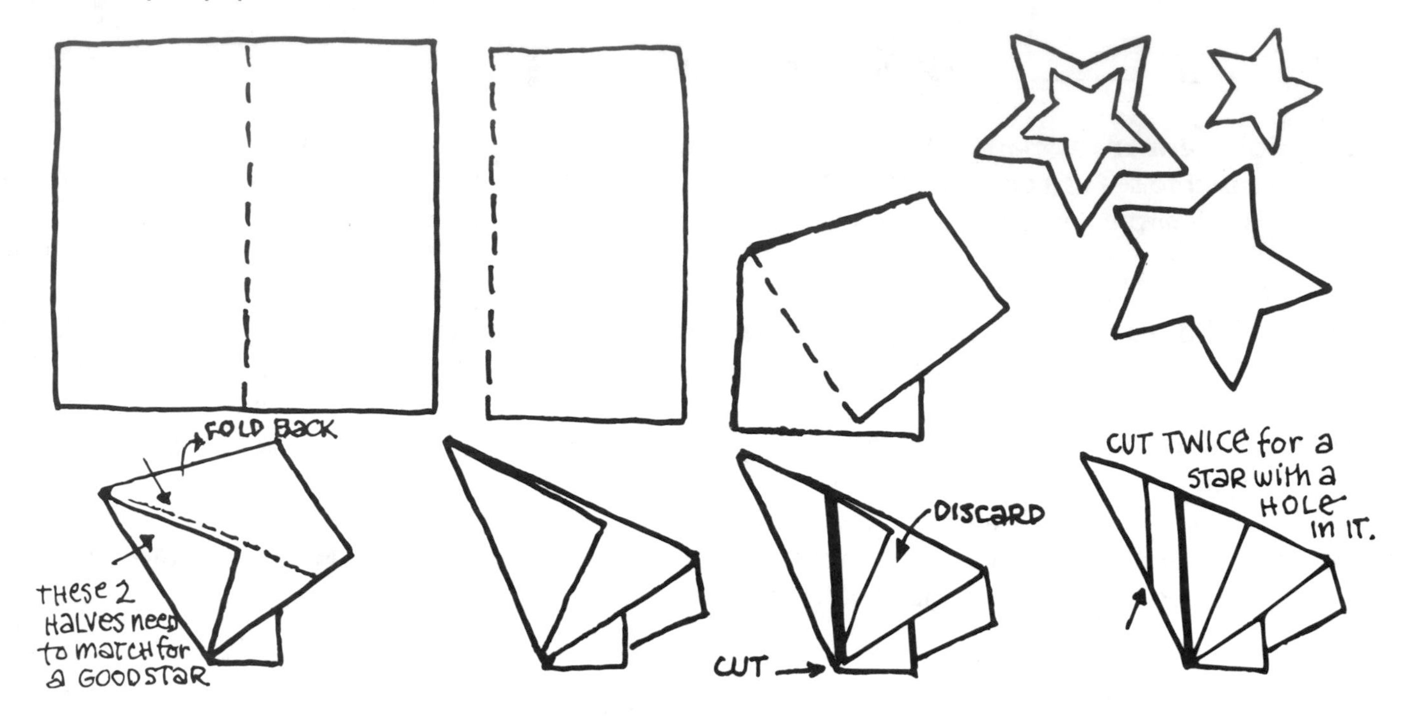


FOLD BACK
THESE 2 HALVES NEED TO MATCH FOR A GOOD STAR

CUT TWICE for a STAR with a HOLE in IT.

**Cat-stair Spring**—This little spring is easy to learn—even in kindergarten, if you go slowly— and it's versatile. The trick is to **fold the strips without lifting them off the table.** As soon as the kids pick them up they start folding **under** instead of **over**, and—well, you'll see. Each child needs two colors of 1″ x 9" or 1″ x 12" strips of construction or colored copier paper to learn the technique.

FOLD ONE STRIP OVER THE OTHER···· FOLD THEM AS FAR AS THEY WILL GO
CONTINUE FOLDING UNTIL THE PAPER IS USED UP. GLUE AT THE TOP TO KEEP THE SPRING FROM COMING APART.
POP-UP PICTURES and GREETING CARDS
SCULPTURES
HANGING DECORATIONS
Be Mine

**Printer's Hat**—My Uncle Herm worked for a newspaper, and he taught all of his nieces and nephews how to make this hat that pressmen wear to keep the ink out of their hair. They use newsprint, but any lightweight paper will work as long as it is as big as a double page of the newspaper. For small children, use smaller paper. Older children (grades 3–5) can learn the folds and make hats for the kindergartners' play area.

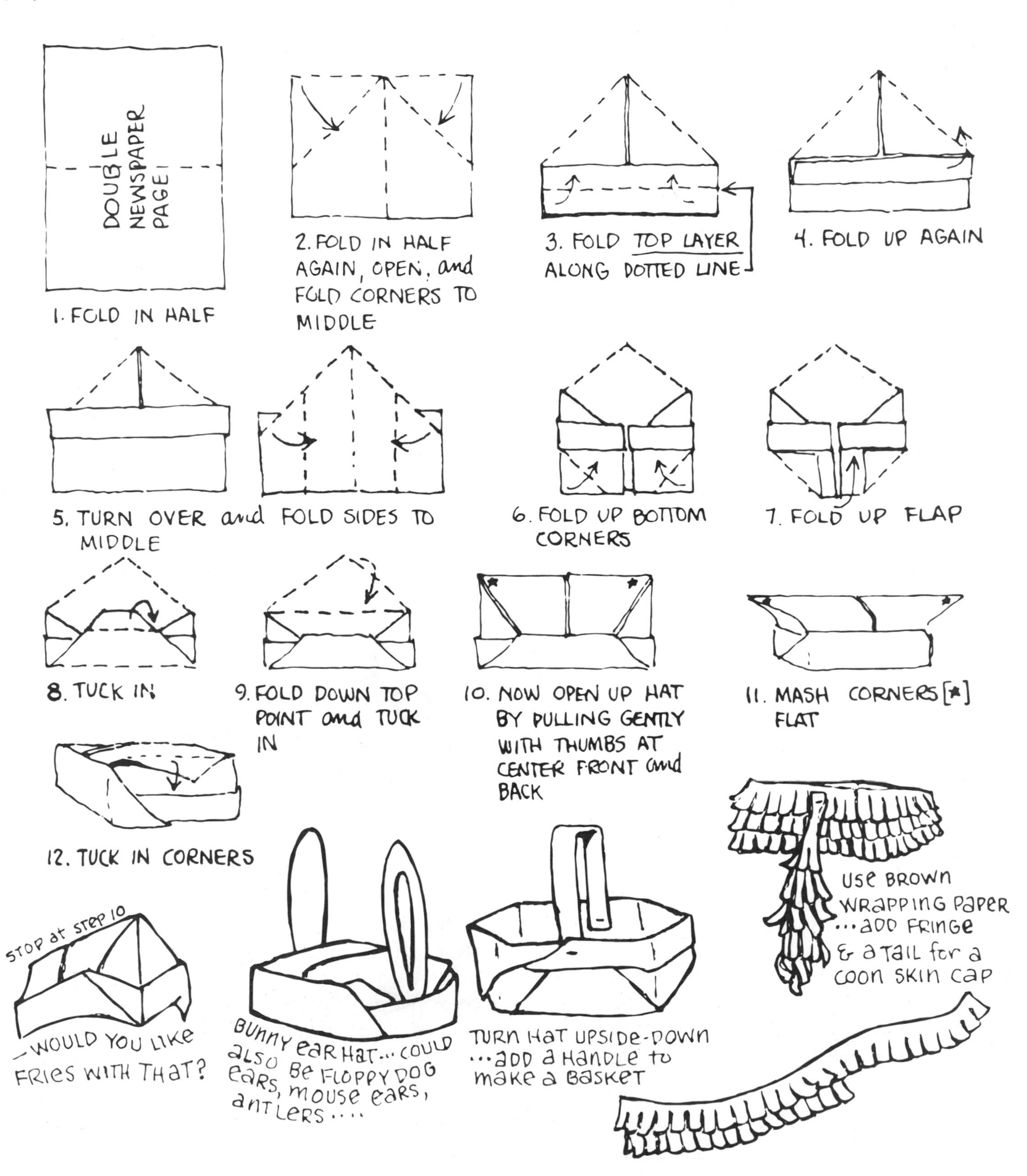

DOUBLE NEWSPAPER PAGE
1. FOLD IN HALF
2. FOLD IN HALF AGAIN, OPEN, and FOLD CORNERS TO MIDDLE
3. FOLD TOP LAYER ALONG DOTTED LINE
4. FOLD UP AGAIN
5. TURN OVER and FOLD SIDES TO MIDDLE
6. FOLD UP BOTTOM CORNERS
7. FOLD UP FLAP
8. TUCK IN
9. FOLD DOWN TOP POINT and TUCK IN
10. NOW OPEN UP HAT BY PULLING GENTLY WITH THUMBS AT CENTER FRONT and BACK
11. MASH CORNERS [*] FLAT
12. TUCK IN CORNERS
STOP at STEP 10
—WOULD YOU LIKE FRIES WITH THAT?
BUNNY EAR HAT... COULD ALSO BE FLOPPY DOG EARS, MOUSE EARS, ANTLERS....
TURN HAT UPSIDE-DOWN ...ADD A HANDLE TO MAKE A BASKET
USE BROWN WRAPPING PAPER ...ADD FRINGE & A TAIL FOR A COON SKIN CAP


 

# Watercolor Tips*

Watercolor is a versatile medium which can be used alone or in combination with other media. For children to have success with watercolor, you need to *teach* them. Read through the suggestions. It would be a good idea to set aside some time to discuss, demonstrate, and try a technique before starting a particular project. Follow up with reminders every time you paint. Students will develop confidence and skill as they get used to using their watercolors.

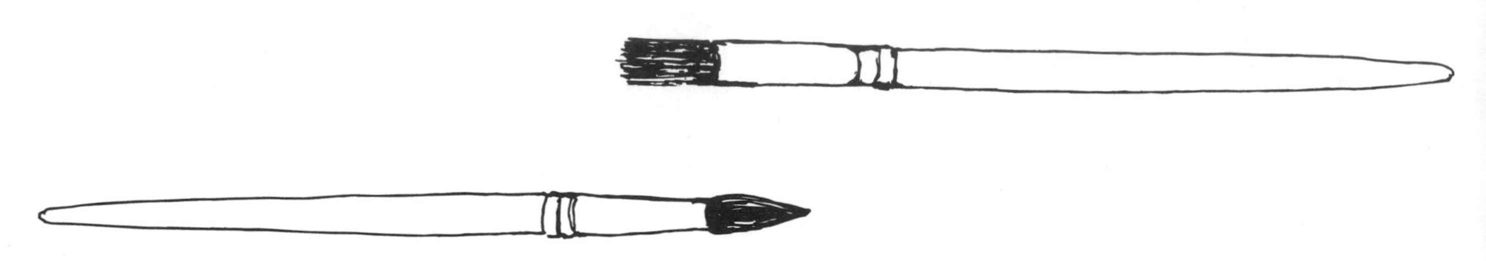

**All about watercolors:** Have students work along with you through this initial "how to" lesson.

**1) How to Clean Your Watercolors**

Get an old box of watercolors that have been put away dirty, or dirty up a box yourself for this demonstration. Some children want to keep their watercolors looking like new. The only way for that to happen is to not use them! Running the whole box under a faucet is counterproductive—good paint goes down the drain, too, and you've got a wet paint box to deal with. This simple method is easy even for the lower grades. **Script:** Your watercolor set has eight colors. If you need more colors, you can get them by mixing. You may be tempted to run your wet brush back and forth across all the colors. BAD IDEA. [Show the dirty paint box]. You will spend all your time cleaning. **For now mix only two colors together at a time**.

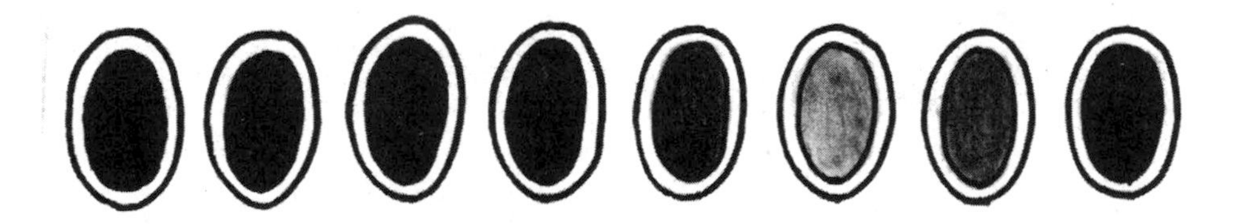

I'm going to show you how to use your brush to clean the paint pans. [**Demonstrate** dipping your brush in the water and wiping a dirty pan. You may have to rinse and wipe a couple of times. For the last wipe, squeeze the water out of the brush and hold it in the pan as you make a slurping noise to indicate that, like a sponge, the brush is soaking up the puddle in the paint. Show how to wipe out the lid, which doubles as a mixing tray. Using a clean, wet brush, swish over the dirty area, then wipe with a paper towel. If the paint pans are very wet after use, let them sit on a counter with the lid open for awhile.] If you want to mix two colors, you can mix right in the pans or put a dab of one color in the mixing tray. Rinse the brush, get a dab of the other color, and add it to the first. Your watercolor sets will get messy once you use them, but you saw that it's not hard to clean the pans. By using a wet brush, you can wipe them clean even if the paint has dried.

**2) How to Use a Brush:** It takes practice to learn how much water to use and how to hold the brush for drawing as well as painting. Even young students can develop this skill if you teach them. Dip the brush in the water and show the class how a watercolor brush is designed to come to a point. **Script:** We are used to using pencils when we draw. What happens if you press hard on your pencil? [Marks get darker. Using black paint show what happens when you press on the brush.] To draw with your brush you need to practice two things: 1) holding it straight up and down, about halfway down the handle, and 2) using a light touch, letting the tip of the brush glide across the paper like a skater on ice. With practice you'll learn just how much water to use—too much, and the lines run; too little, and the lines are scratchy. As the brush dries out, dip **just the tip** in the water, add a little more paint, and you're good to go. It's okay to gently reshape the brush with your fingers.

to REFRESH the point DIP JUST the TIP in the WATER....
I'm DROWNING!


**3) I don't have any pink! How to make light colors**

Although some watercolor sets include a white pan, most do not. To lighten a color, use water. **Script:** Suppose you want to paint something lavender. What color would you use? [violet or purple] I'm wetting my brush and painting—oh no, this is **too** purple! No problem. I can **blot** it with a paper towel **or** rinse my brush and **add a little water** —a few swishes will lighten up the color. You can also **rinse and squeeze** the water out of the brush to **soak up** the too-dark color.

...ADD WATER
OR... SOAK UP WITH BRUSH

**4) How to WAIT!**
Students need to learn to "skip around" when they paint with watercolors. Painting on or very close to wet paint will cause the colors to run together. [There's a scientific principle at work here.] **Script:** I'm painting a yellow ball. I want to make a funny face on the ball, so I'll rinse and blot my brush, then paint black eyes. [As you demonstrate this, the kids will get the point as the black bleeds all over the yellow.] **If you paint on a wet area, the colors will run.** I should have waited for the yellow to dry before I painted the eyes. Even if you get *close* to a wet color, the two colors can run together. Should you just sit there while you're waiting? What *could* you do? Yes, you could paint another area of your picture, then come back and finish what you started when the paint dries. I'm going to paint some more yellow ball heads while I wait. By the time I'm done, the first one should be dry. If it isn't quite dry, I'll blot it—gently!

## Other Techniques to Try

**Wet-on-wet: Use good white drawing or manila paper.** Have extra, smaller sheets for experimenting. There are times when you *want* colors to run. For instance, if you're doing a unit on weather, kinds of clouds, sunrise/sunset, you might have the class paint skies. In this case you would start with the background color(s), then in another session add details to the dry sky-scapes with crayon, oil crayon, markers, cut paper, or a combination. Try this yourself before you demonstrate. It's not a technique that you can control, but by experimenting you'll see how it works. The biggest problem is the tendency to go too far, ending up with **muddy colors**. Another approach is to squeeze brush loads of wet colors onto the wet paper, letting them spread and mingle, to create a background for any number of picture themes—circus, fireworks, flower garden, birthday party.

**Black crayon and watercolor—Black Sharpie permanent marker and watercolor**
The addition of black lines to watercolor paintings helps define the colors and images. Watercolor artists draw lines with their brushes, but this can be frustrating for young painters.
**Black crayon** works best **before** painting and actually helps contain the paint. **Black Sharpie permanent marker** works before or after. Don't use marker until the paint is dry.

**Crayon resist**
Use watercolors to fill in spaces in crayon drawings. Crayon is applied heavily so the wax will repel the wet paint. Bring science into a crayon resist project by asking students why it works.
Also see pages 56, 100–102.

*I recommend Prang Watercolors Sets (eight colors in oval pans) for elementary students. The colors are bright, mix well, and work better than any other brand in **crayon resist** projects. NOTE: Prang **Washable** Watercolor Sets are better than most *inexpensive* watercolors, but not as versatile as regular Prangs, and not refillable.

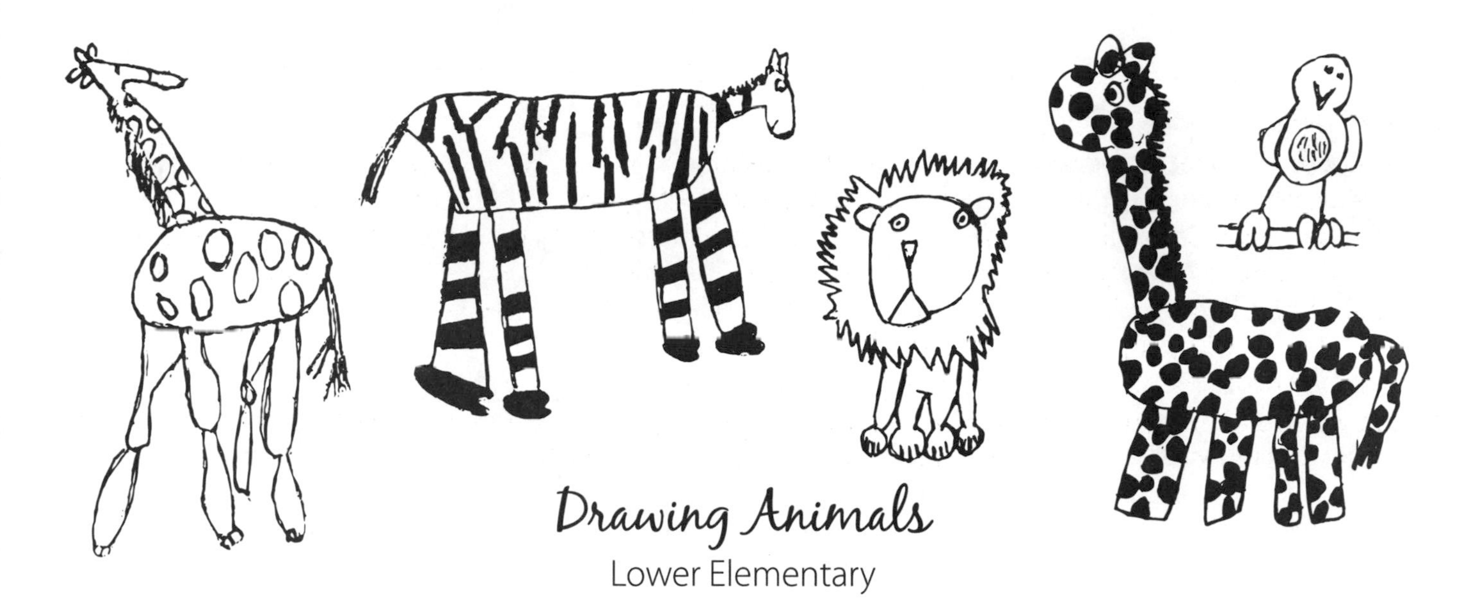

# Drawing Animals

Lower Elementary

Children in the primary grades tend to draw "the whole thing," head to toe (snout to tail). Artists generally sketch out the shapes of each part of the subject. It's hard for students to understand this because we rarely see evidence of the steps taken to arrive at the finished work. Lead your students through the following demonstration to teach them how to draw an animal by carefully observing and drawing each part. The ideal experience is to draw from observation, but since that isn't always possible, the method discussed here relies on good photographs for inspiration. The same ideas apply—noticing the shapes of the parts, starting with big shapes, and finishing with the little details.

Before you begin, put up (nature calendar) photographs of the animal(s) you are going to draw. Try to find front and side views of the animals. Put up a sheet of paper for your demonstration. The only supplies needed are newsprint or copier paper, pencils, and erasers. Make sure everybody can see what you're doing.

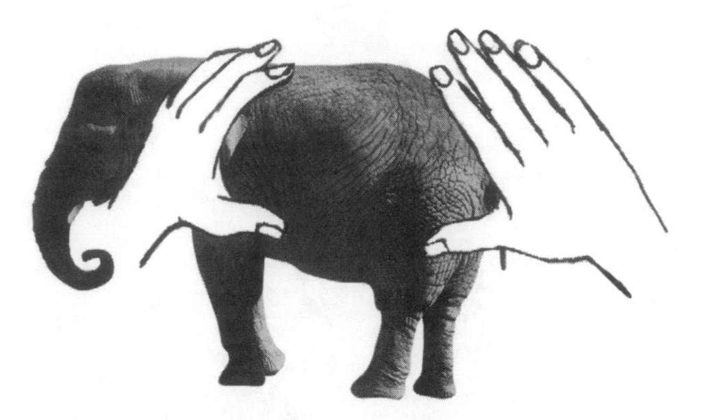

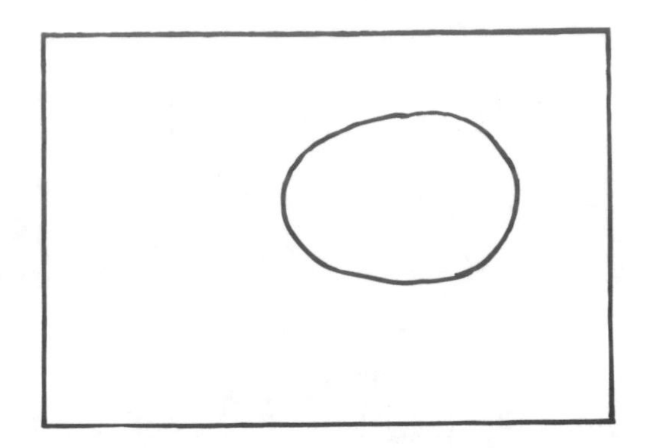

**Example:** Placing your hands around the body of the elephant, isolating that shape, ask students to name the shape that comes closest to the body shape. [Answers may not be what you anticipate. For instance, a child may say the body of an elephant looks like a rectangle. Here's where comparisons work. A giraffe's body really is rectangular. By *comparison* what shape is the elephant's body? Rounder or ovalish.] Draw a fairly large elephant body on your paper, and encourage children to do likewise, making sure to leave room for heads, trunks, and legs.

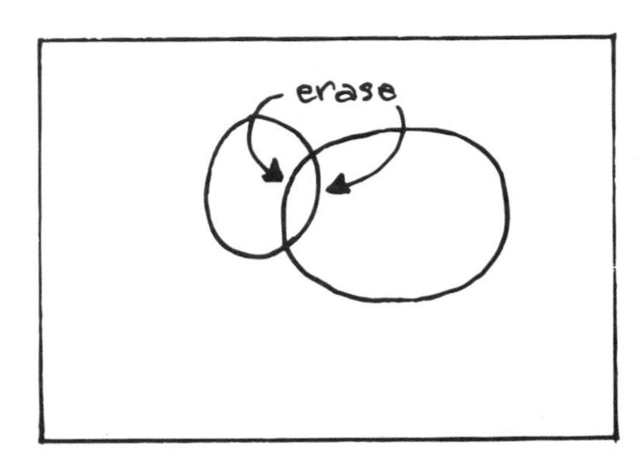


Next, isolate the head, noticing its shape and that it sticks up a bit higher than the body. Is there any neck? No, the head really seems to overlap the body a bit. Draw the head, overlapping, then erase the overlapping lines. Continue the process of naming shapes, drawing and erasing, until the animal is finished. Some things, like the elephant's trunk or giraffe's neck, are not simple shapes. In those cases, compare them to something—"an elephant's trunk looks like a ______." Or describe the way the part looks—the giraffe's neck is wider where it joins the body and narrower close to the head.

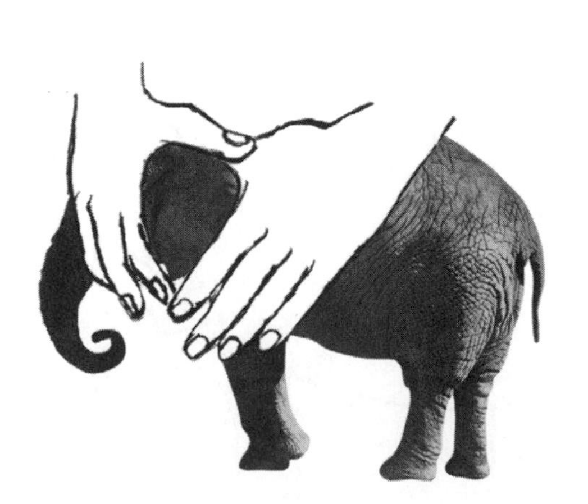

Animal Sketches*... Jungle Animals
HELP! I'm tipping over...
What's with these legs?
Legs are attached at front & back
Elephants on the move! Extend the lines on near legs to accentuate overlap
Hose-like trunks & tails
Horns on top-ears @ back
Triangular head
short mane
Knobby knees
what shape are giraffe spots?
RHINO-kidney beans
Start with a face...
G-R-R-R-R
—Look at the monkey's long arms & tail.... big ears—no neck
FARM Animals
A cow is boxy
Oink!
A pig has a snout, curly tail, split hooves & an oink!
Start with a big cloud & a little cloud

★ **SHOW** YOUR STUDENTS BASIC TECHNIQUES, THEN ENJOY THEIR **PERSONAL** INTERPRETATIONS.

# Drawing Animals

Upper Elementary—4th & 5th

Students at this level are a mixed bag in their drawing abilities. The difference between them and lower elementary students is their awareness of and interest in naturalism or realism. Some students may be exceptionally perceptive, skillful drawers.*

Drawing is all about **believing what you <u>see</u>, not what you <u>know</u>.** Anybody can make marks on paper, but putting them down in the right way is another thing. Artists analyze relationships and trust their eyes. This is a skill that can be learned with practice. The most useful piece of advice for young drawers is, "Draw lightly at first and plan to use your eraser!" Even accomplished artists draw and redraw.

Favorite animals among this age group may be influenced in part by studies of the rain forest and endangered species. You may also notice that girls like horses, dolphins, cute, cuddly dogs, pandas, and baby seals, while boys tend to prefer wolves, deer, panthers, tree frogs.

At this level you can give students more choices, but as a rule some parameters make for better results. In lower elementary you'll get better results if you dictate paper size and color and the medium (pencil, crayon, marker), leaving the choice of animal up to the student. While it may not always be possible for various reasons, know that older students are capable of determining the **format** (rectangle, square, circle), type of **paper** (white drawing, colored construction), and **size**, they would like to use, then choosing from several **media** which they have at their seats or that you have made available. Most fourth and fifth graders like a medium they can control. Colored pencils are popular. Watercolors, NOT.

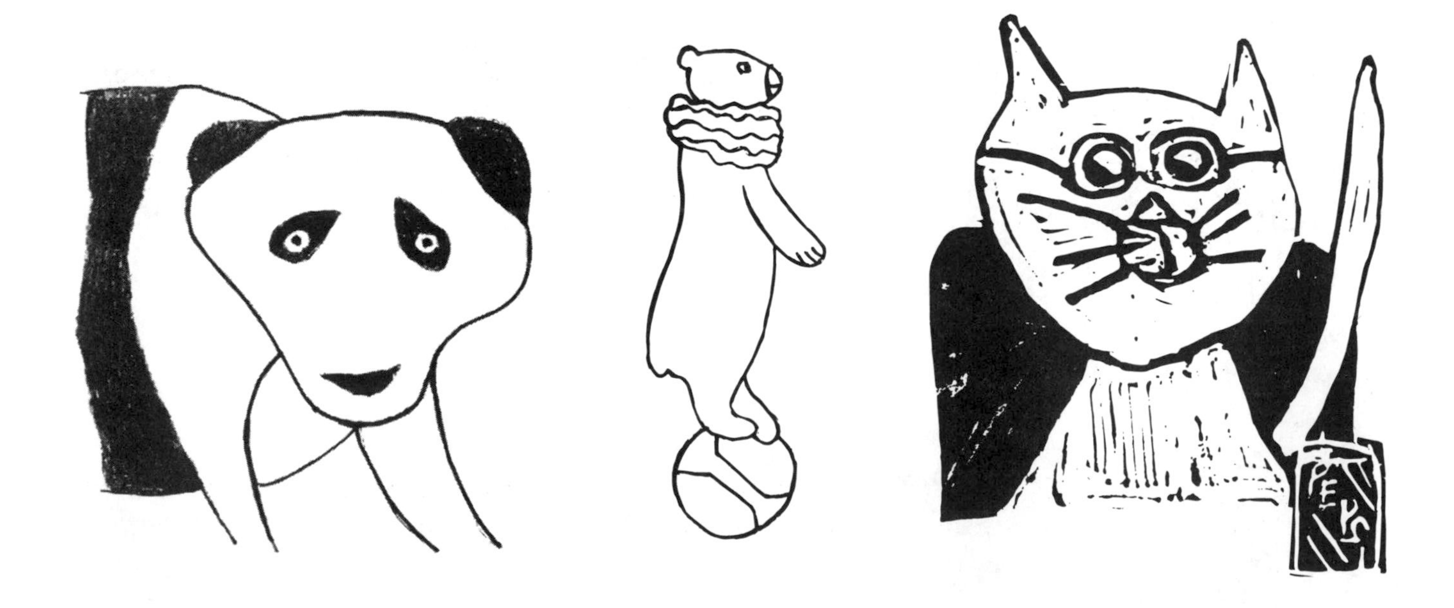

*These students sometimes balk if you ask them to paint or use any medium that won't allow the detail they can get with pencil. It doesn't hurt to force them out of their comfort zone from time to time.

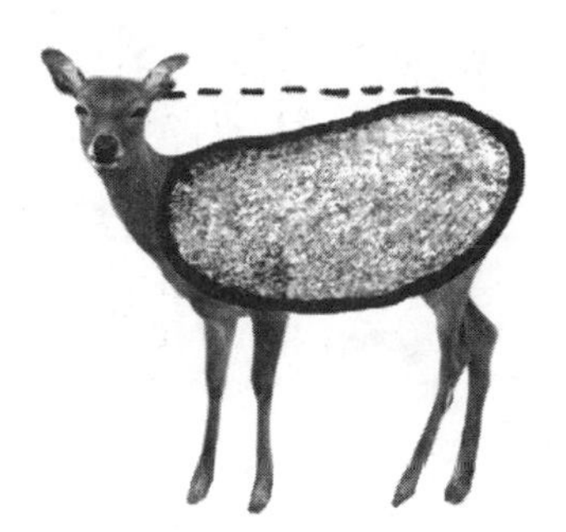

[This is a sample to show you how to help your students go about drawing an animal from a photograph, where to start and what to look for.] Notice that the body of the deer tilts up at the rear. The dotted line indicates that the head (just below the ears) is even with the rear. Draw the body shape.

Next, pay attention to that pretty little curve joining the neck to the top of the body. Draw it. Then draw the other side of the neck, a gentler curve, joining the lower body.

The head is quite small. Here's where the light guideline will help you get it in the right position with respect to the rear. Draw the head and add eyes, nose, and ears.

Before drawing the legs, study the shape of the **space between the legs**. That helps you get them positioned. Notice how the back leg joins the body with a curve. The lower leg is straight, angles toward the front, and gets narrower at the foot. Paying attention to the shape of that space, draw the front leg.

Draw the other two legs, again using the shapes of the spaces between the two front legs and the two back legs to help you see where to put them.

Remember! Drawing is personal. It's **your interpretation** of what you see. If you want a picture that's exactly right in every way, use a camera!

CHECK HOW EYES & EARS LINE UP
EYES FLAT ACROSS TOP
WIDER CHEEK THIS SIDE
HEART-SHAPED NOSE & SNOUT
TRIANGULAR EARS
TIPS OF EARS HANG LOWER than eyes
FROM A CALENDAR PHOTO
TRIANGLES
REAR SLANTS UP
SHAPE OF THE SPACE BETW. HEAD & REAR
SHAPES OF EMPTY (NEGATIVE) SPACES!
STUDENT GALLERY

# *Animals in a Border*

Grade 5

**Supplies:** pencil, eraser, sketch paper (sketchbooks or clean backs of recycled paper), white drawing paper, 9″ x 9" and 9" x 12", straightedge, colored pencils, crayons, colored and black Sharpie permanent markers, photographs of animals (calendar pics, wildlife magazines, choosing photos that fit with your unit of study—jungle, rain forest, pets, endangered species), examples of animal drawings and paintings from realistic to stylized to cartoony.

**Suggested artists**: Albrecht Dürer, M.C. Escher, aborigine, Mexican, and African folk art, children's book illustrators—Lois Ehlert, Eric Carle, David Weisner; *The Eleventh Hour* (art with borders) by Graeme Base, *The Peaceable Kingdom* by Alice and Martin Provensen, *Animal Shapes* by Brian Wildsmith

**Preparation:** Several days before you begin the project, allow students to choose one or more photographs from which to sketch. If you allow them to take the work home, make sure they bring it and the photos back before you introduce the lesson.

**Motivation:** Show the class several examples of animals drawn by artists and illustrators. Ask students to describe the differences they see in styles. Is one style better than another? Does art have to hang on a wall in a museum or appear in a book to make it **ART**? How about the art of groups like the aborigines of Australia? What does their art mean to them? What is there to like about it? [This conversation should help students understand that there are many approaches to art and prepare them to experiment bravely! Don't expect 100% cooperation here, but if a couple of students are getting good results, their work may motivate others.]

**Assignment: 1)** Use the straightedge to rule off a 1" border around the paper, then draw a stylized animal using one of your sketches as a starting point. This may mean simplifying, cartooning, leaving out some details while adding others, using color creatively. [Show examples from books above and others with stylized illustrations. Find examples of animals in aborigine, Mexican, Native American, and African art]. **2)** Design the border to complement the animal. (Have examples of borders available for ideas.) **3)** Your choice of media—crayons, colored pencils, markers, or a combination

# Butterflies

Grades 2–5

**Supplies:** 12" x 18" white drawing or pastel-colored construction paper; yellow chalkboard chalk; erasers; crayons; color photos of butterflies*

**Part I—Discussion:** (Post pictures of mostly butterflies and a couple of moths.) Ask students to describe the **differences** they see between butterflies and moths.) Moths—feathery antennae, more neutral colors, browns and grays; butterflies—smooth, long antennae, bright colors, lots of spots and stripes) **Script:** How many wings does a butterfly have? [Four, 2 upper, 2 lower] What shape are the wings? [For the most part the upper wings are triangular; bottom wings are shaped somewhat like a slice of pie.] Where do the wings hook onto a butterfly's body? [Older students may say "thorax"; younger, "in the middle"—no matter what the age level, use the teachable moment to name the parts, "head, thorax, and abdomen."] Butterflies are symmetrical. What does that mean? [The two halves match.] The photographs are mostly [depending on what you use] specimens that have been laid out flat. Their wings match, because they're not in motion. But when a butterfly is fluttering around, the wings may not look exactly the same shape on both sides. Don't worry about perfectly matching wings. Notice how the wings go up much higher than the top of the head and lower than the bottom of the abdomen. (This is not true of all butterflies.) Is there any space between the top and bottom wings? [No—they overlap.] Try this motion along with me. It'll help you when you start to draw. [Put your index fingers together, then, with a full arm motion, take them up and out as if tracing the tops of the wings—then describe the sides and bottom, bringing your fingers back together.]

**Demonstration:** Put up a paper (a color that shows the chalk well) and ask for a volunteer to draw the body of a butterfly. Then, repeating the air-drawing motion, ask someone to draw the top wings and another volunteer to draw bottom wings. Call attention to the length of the antennae and have someone add them.

**Assignment:** Draw a large butterfly. Encourage students to make the butterflies look alive by perching them on a flower or tilting them as if in flight. They may want to make more than one butterfly.

Pass out chalk, let students choose paper, and let the butterfly drawing begin!

**Part II: Discussion/ Demonstration:** [Now the attention is focused on color and pattern.] When most of the drawings are finished, gather the class around the sample drawing. They need to be close to see the crayon technique. **Script:** Notice the colors on the wings, how they seem to melt into each other. As you look at the pictures, you find that some butterflies are mostly one color with a few stripes or spots, while others have many patterns all over their wings. I'll demonstrate a way to blend colors to get that soft, butterfly-wing look. I will be coloring around the patterns and working from the body out to the edges of the wings. First I'm going to choose a color "family" from the crayon box. What **is** a color family? Colors that look related! [Hold up orange, yellow, yellow-orange, red-orange, and blue]. Which color isn't a member of this family—not even a distant cousin? [blue, of course] What do all the other colors have in common? [the colors red and yellow] **Demonstrate the technique:** with red-orange, color a top wing outward from the body a couple of inches. Switch to orange. Overlap the first color and continue coloring outward, going around the patterns and pressing firmly. Repeat with yellow-orange and yellow, each time coloring back over the previous color. You can keep going or leave room for a contrasting color around the edges. Point out that top and bottom wings don't necessarily match, but left and right wings do. If you're working with younger students, you can expect more variety of outcomes. Don't be rigid—enjoy their originality. Older students will have more understanding of the technique and interest in a realistic approach.

**One more thing!** The butterflies will have a good buildup of wax if students have pressed and colored layer on layer. You can polish it! Using tissue or toilet paper (artists use whatever works) show how to gently buff the crayon, stressing that now a **light touch** is needed to keep from smearing the colors.

*There are many books and calendars featuring butterflies. I found this one on a book store discount table. It's beautiful: *Butterflies and Moths of the World*, Alain Eid and Michel Viard, Chartwell Book, a division of Book Sales, Inc. 1997

 

# *Rain Forests, Jungles, and Henri Rousseau*

Grades 1–2

This lesson can be adapted to different media, depending on how much time you have to spend. The one described here is a four-part cut paper collage. **Refer to the section on drawing animals, page 16.**

**Supplies:** 6″ x 9" construction paper in animal colors (gray, orange, white, black, brown, yellow); 12" x 18" construction paper in light blue, black, and yellow; a couple shades of green paper 4 ½″ x 6" and 2″ x 18" strips; pencils, scissors, glue, crayons, scrap box paper; magazine and calendar photos of jungle animals and flowers, **folder for each child;** Rousseau **reproductions** *Surprise!* or *Exotic Landscape* **or** the book described below.

NOTE: Animal skin paper, available in arts and crafts catalogs can make this project extra special.

**Background on Henri Rousseau:** born in France, 1844; took up painting at forty-nine, with no formal training; was fascinated with jungle plants and animals—visited greenhouses and zoos for inspiration. The book ***A Weekend with Rousseau***, Gilles Plazy, Rizzoli, N.Y., is beautifully illustrated with Rousseau jungles and other works. There is some nudity, so it may not be appropriate for the classroom bookshelf!

What better way to introduce students to an artist who loved all aspects of the jungle than to include this project in a study of the rain forest! As students learn about the layers of the forest, the flora and fauna, through Rousseau's work, they can also learn to appreciate the sheer beauty of it all. By working on one thing at a time, you will actually be teaching several different techniques and skills over a period of four weeks. The weeks will be broken down like this: 1) animals 2) background trees and bushes 3) flowers and grasses 4) creating the jungle scene.

**Art Motivation, Week 1: (animal colors)** Look at a couple of examples of Rousseau jungle scenes and ask students to name what they see. Explain that they will be working on one thing at a time, beginning with animals. Have lots of animal photos tacked up or available for students to take to their seats. **Demonstrate** how to draw an animal part by part on the construction paper or the *back* of the animal skin paper. The drawing marks will not be visible on the front. Another approach is to cut out the parts and assemble with glue. Demonstrate this. Spots, stripes, manes, features can be added with crayon. Save the work in the folders, which will be added to each week.

3
2
5
6
1
4
4
ADD DETAILS WITH CRAYON
ANOTHER WAY....
...CUT OUT THE PARTS & GLUE THEM TOGETHER
ANY TIME YOU'RE CUTTING MULTIPLES, DOUBLE UP THE PAPER!


**Week 2: (tree colors)** Again, look at a jungle scene, this time focusing on the trees, noticing that they sometimes go clear off the top of the picture. Ask how jungle trees are different from the trees in the neighborhood. (Of course if you live in a jungle-like climate, they may not be all that different.) Look at the shapes of the leaves and the way they are attached to the branches. Using the tree colors, **demonstrate** how to cut branches and attach them to a trunk and how to fold over the paper to cut lots of leaves. Allow finished trees to dry before putting them in the folders.

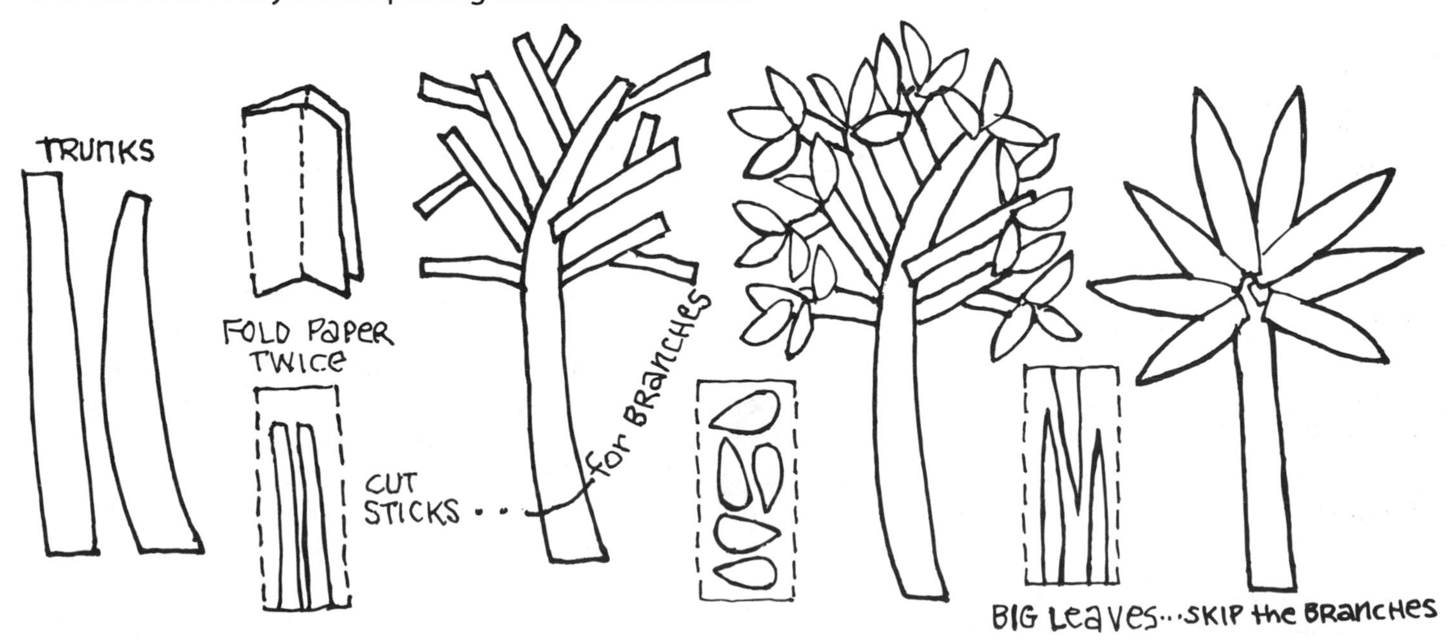

FOLD PAPER TWICE
CUT STICKS...
for BRANCHES
BIG LEAVES...SKIP THE BRANCHES

**Week 3: (flower colors from scrap paper and grass strips)** If you have no scraps, tear up some bright papers in reds, pinks, and yellows, and white. This time notice the flowers in Rousseau's work. The flowers and fruits break up the monotony of all that green. **Demonstrate** ways to cut flower petals and how to fold and cut the green strips to make grass cutting a breeze. Allow glue to dry before storing.

**Week 4: (scraps from the preceding weeks and the large sheets of construction paper) Script:** [Looking at the Rousseau] Notice that the sky seems to be in the back, behind everything else. What is *just* in front of the sky? (trees) What do you find in the middle? (animals, tall grass, flowers, bushes) And very close? (more grass, flowers, animal(s), maybe another tall tree) **Demonstrate:** Lay sheets of each of the large colored papers on the floor in front of you and have the class form a large semicircle around you, so students watch what you're doing. Use your own sample folder or borrow one from a class member to show your students how to experiment with all of the various parts and arrange them into a composition. Place the tall trees near or touching the top of the paper, allowing the color of the background to show through. Next play around with animals, bushes, grass, and flowers. Overlap these elements to show things behind and in front of each other. Another layer of grass might go along the bottom of the paper.

If there are gaps between the tall grasses where the background color shows through, use crayon to fill it in. Ask students what effect the background color has. (Which one looks hot? fair and mild? like night?) They should think before choosing. When they have finished arranging their compositions, they should carefully glue the pieces down. Hang and enjoy!

The example shown here gives you an idea of the drawn jungle, using pencil, black Sharpie permanent marker, and crayon. The motivation and demonstration should come after you've practiced sketching animals as described on page 17. In your demonstration, model drawing lightly, because erasures will happen. Work from foreground to background, starting at the bottom of the page and working up. Demonstrate how to show "in front and behind," even though some won't be ready for that concept. When the drawing is complete, use black Sharpie permanent marker to trace over lines. Encourage strong color application. The sky can be colored to look hot, rainy, sunset, night…or painted with wet watercolors.

# Drawing from Careful Observation

Grades 3–5

Sometimes careful drawing is required. This lesson fosters the kind of accurate renderings found in science books. A conversation with students before beginning helps them appreciate why sometimes the creative "anything goes" approach will not do. Take advanced medical texts, for instance. Would we want future surgeons to be studying creative interpretations of the brain, heart, kidneys or any other body part? Making this point is important to set the stage for the drawing activity. It may persuade the "I can't draw" students to give it a serious try. The works of Albrecht Dürer and M. C. Escher are inspiring examples of careful observation.

**Supplies:** white copier paper, magnifying glasses, pencils, and erasers. On a table arrange a collection of natural objects—feathers, seashells, broken walnut shells, acorns, pinecones, wheat, flowers, leaves, rocks, butterflies. (Did you know that a reasonably intact butterfly can be laminated? I didn't until I tried it!) **For the demonstration:** overhead projector, black Sharpie permanent marker, clean acetate, damp rag.

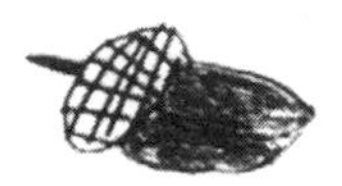

**Demonstration:** You will have to draw for your students. Practice ahead of time. Use the overhead projector. (It took me over 25 years to discover what a great tool this is! First, everybody can see what you're doing. Second, in this project, the shadows of the objects are well-defined). Place a leaf, shell, feather, some wheat or grass on the overhead and let students identify them by their shadows. Point out the irregular edges. Remove all but the feather. To make clear to the students what "careful observation" means, you will make two drawings of the feather. First, draw it as you would if you were not looking at a feather—a typical generic feather. Now for the fun one! Although the students are seeing only the silhouette of the feather, you will carefully draw in the details, beginning with the "shaft." Talk and ask questions as you draw, noticing how this line curves slightly and widens at the bottom (calamus). Tell the students you are drawing slowly and carefully this *particular* feather.

Begin drawing the barbs on either side of the shaft—at this point it is helpful to lightly outline the overall shape, noticing any gaps or ruffles. Can you record every line like a camera? OF COURSE NOT! But you can make a sensitive drawing. Let the children compare the feather silhouette, your "any old feather," and the second, more accurate drawing.

**Directions:** Students will go to the table and choose one object to draw. As they finish, they can trade for a second object, then a third. Let each student decide how to organize the drawing. Some may want to do all shells. Some may line up the objects in a row or make a border. It really doesn't matter. Some may shade with the pencil, while others will use only lines. The important thing is that they take their time. This is not easy work for children who can't concentrate and may repeatedly try to find something "easy" to draw. It's important for them to try! You know your students and can hone in on the ones who need your encouragement. Some of the drawings will amaze you.

**Tips:** Lazy or fearful students may resort to tracing the objects. Some may just not be able to break down the parts to make the drawing easier. The illustrations and comments below should help you get them to focus on basic shapes to get started.

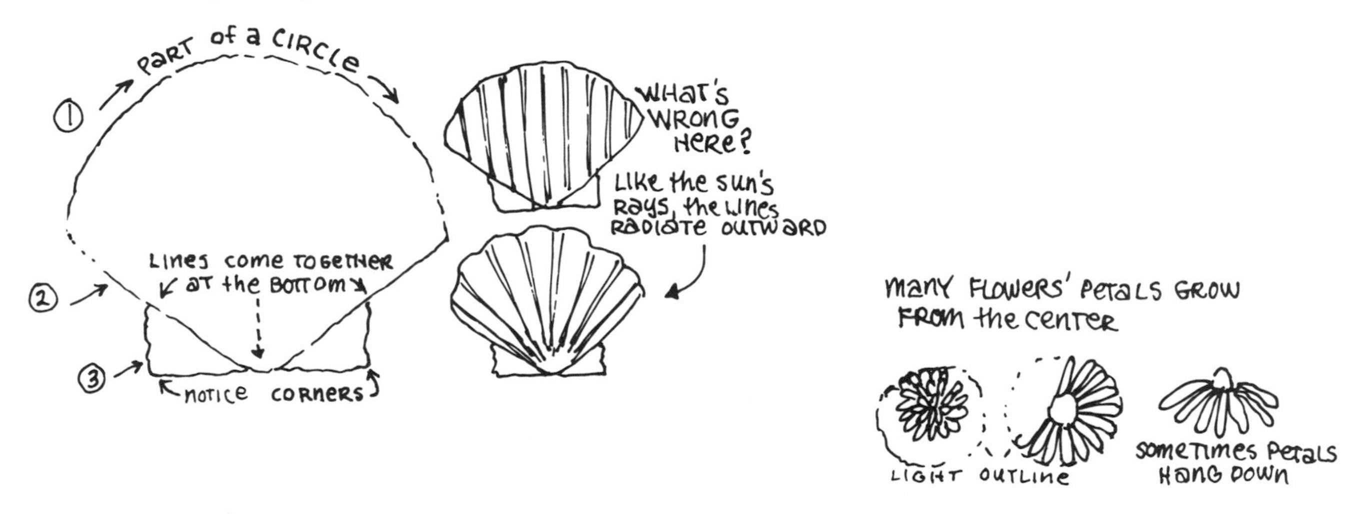


**Display suggestions:** Pencil drawings look good mounted on gray paper. In some cases there may be good drawings on the same page with scribbled-out mistakes. I see nothing wrong with cropping drawings for display. These drawings might be part of a science bulletin board along with nature drawings by artists or photographs from nature magazines.

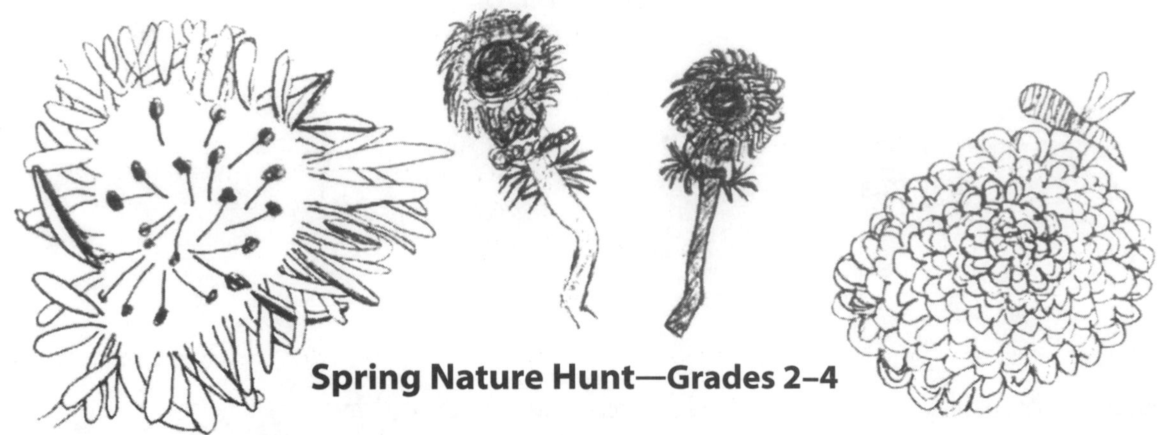

## Spring Nature Hunt—Grades 2–4

**Supplies:** plastic containers, pencils, erasers, copier or white drawing paper (in the 9" x 12" range or half that size, if you prefer), magnifying glasses

Here's another way to approach drawing objects found in nature. Divide students into teams of four. Give each team a container and the following list of things to look for:

| | |
|---|---|
| Something round | Something hard |
| Something rough | Something sharp |
| Something fuzzy, furry, or hairy | Something beautiful |
| Something ugly | Something funny |

Instruct students to work with their teammates to find the items on the list, then go out to the playground. After ten or twelve minutes of running, stooping, shouting, consulting, reconsidering, and filling their containers, go back to the classroom to compare results.

Among other things, you may expect to find rocks, dandelions (in blossom and gone to seed), sharp sticks, evergreen twigs, moss, leaves, violets, insects, dirt, or gravel. One team in a class I worked with found a dead mouse and suggested that it filled ALL the categories!

After the teams have looked at all the collections, hand out magnifying glasses. Each student will pick an object to examine carefully and draw in detail. Display the drawings on a science and nature bulletin board.

**Variation:** Try it in the fall and *again* in the spring. Be sure to save the fall pictures for comparison.

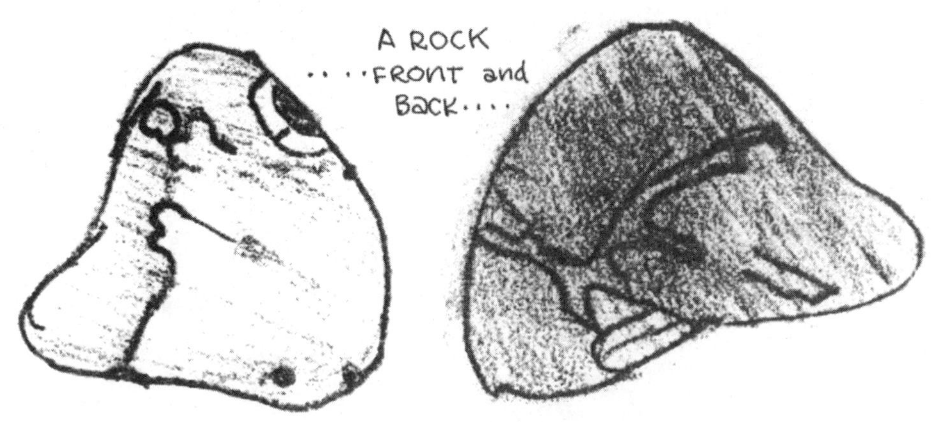

# Skeletons

Grades 1–2

We all have bones! Without getting too technical, this activity helps children understand how our skeletons make us strong and make it possible for us to bend, reach, and twist. It's a good fall project which could tie in with Halloween or the Mexican Day of the Dead celebration.

**Supplies:** construction paper—black (12″ x 18"), white (6″ x 9"), and orange, (6″ x 9"); scissors, glue, black crayon

**Discussion:** Ask students if they have ever noticed bones that are close enough to the skin to be felt. Let them take turns showing where these bones are and have everybody find them on themselves. Some that will be mentioned: wrist, fingers, knees (patella), elbows, head (skull)—yes, we are all boneheads—shins, ankles, back, and ribs. Take a moment to think about **why** our skulls need to be hard and strong and why we have a cage inside our chests. Make sure everybody agrees that bones are rigid and cannot bend.

**Script:** How many bones do you think there are between the shoulder and the hand, one long bone or more than one? Let's suppose there is just one bone all the way from shoulder to wrist. Everybody make a stiff arm. Now pretend to eat a bowl of cereal. What? You can't get the spoon to your mouth? Where do the bones come together. Yes, elbows. **Joints** are places where bones come together, allowing us to bend. [Go through the same routine with legs, by having the children stand and try to sit down without bending their knees.] What do we call all the bones put together? Yes, skeleton.

**Demonstration:** Tape a piece of black paper on the board. Cut out a head shape from the white paper and glue it to the paper. (This shape doesn't have to resemble a real skull—round or oval is fine. If a child wants to make a skull shape, it helps to think "light bulb.") Now demonstrate a quick and easy way to cut bones by holding the white paper horizontally and cutting strips from bottom to top. Having a little pile of strips to start with is more efficient. The strips can then be cut to whatever length needed. Glue a strip below the skull to represent the back bone, and glue 3–4 short strips across it for ribs. This is one time when it's easier to put the glue on the background paper. Show how to draw a thin thread of glue where a bone will be placed.

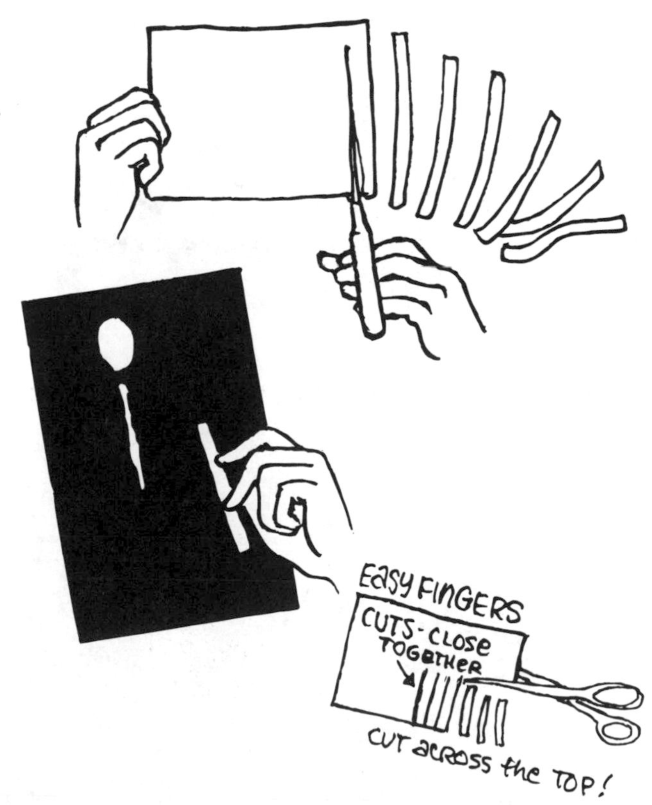


 

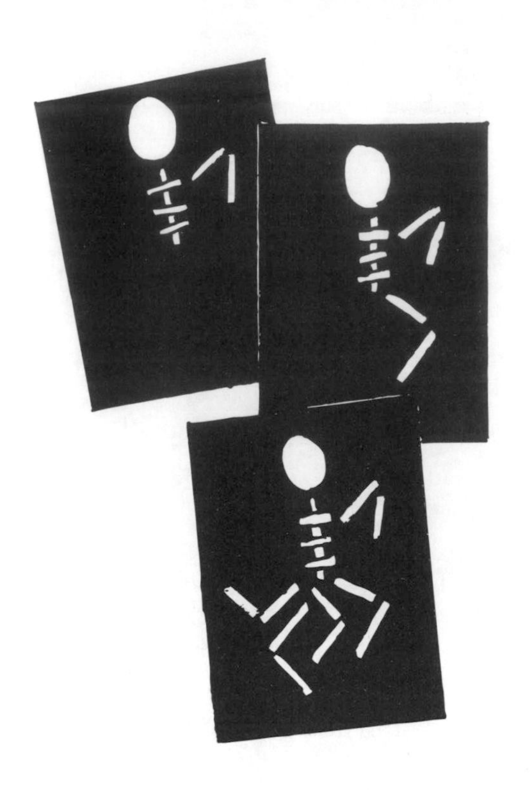

Now ask for a volunteer to use **two** bones to make **one** bent arm. Bend your own arms in different ways, to illustrate. (If the student tries to use the strips to make two arms, repeat the instructions.) Repeat the process with the legs. After one leg is in place, hold two other strips up to the example to show how running, jumping, or dancing legs might look. Remind everyone to begin by cutting strips, then gluing on head, backbone, and ribs first. Remove the example from the board, and ask students what they could do with the orange paper. Some might want to use it for the skeleton's skull, while most will make jack-o'-lanterns, using the black crayon to draw features on both jack-o'-lanterns and skull.

As the period progresses, keep restating the rule: two bones for each arm and two for each leg. Some children may want to make more than one skeleton on the page. Encourage the addition of finger bones and feet. Make an eye-catching Halloween bulletin board by overlapping the papers, leaving no gaps in the black. Although this lesson is primarily a fun holiday activity, it is not trite and does teach a rudimentary anatomy lesson. As you have students draw figures throughout the year, remind them of the dancing skeletons to encourage arm and leg action.

For fun, challenge each student to try to get in the same position as the skeleton (s)he created.

# *Silhouettes and Watercolor Skies*

Grades 4–5

**Supplies:** 12" x 18" white drawing or manila paper, pencils, black crayons or **permanent** black markers (large Sharpie), watercolors, water containers, table or desk covers, calendar photos and/ or other visuals of landscapes, cityscapes, or seascapes **at sunset**; *Silhouettes, A Pictorial Archive of Varied Illustrations,* edited by Carol Belanger Grafton,1979, Dover Publications, Inc.

**Part I**

**Discussion/ Motivation:** (Post visuals where everyone can see them.) **Script:** What do all the pictures have in common? [silhouetted images] How can you identify the objects? [by shape] Why do colors disappear at sunset? What is needed to see color? [light] When light shines on an object, we see its color. When the sun is low in the sky, we can see the shapes of trees and buildings but no color. At a certain point, when the sun rises high enough, we see color; at a certain point, when the sun goes down, we see no color. Why do we still see the windows when a building is in silhouette? [This project would reinforce the study of light and optics in science class.]

**Demonstration:** (Your demonstration might reflect the area in which you live or a region you are studying.) Draw a ground line (or sky line), then add whatever buildings, trees, birds, animals you want. Keep it simple. Using black marker, color some part of the drawing that particularly emphasizes shape. (If using crayon, demonstrate how to color heavily for a good, dark black.) **Script:** Since we are drawing silhouettes, we can't show details like bricks and shutters. To make an interesting picture, we have to concentrate on shapes—the shapes of trees with bare branches, the shapes of buildings (see illustrations).

## Part II

**Demonstration:** [see page 14] When most of the class has finished the first part, gather students around to demonstrate the watercolor sky technique. **[Try this before demonstrating.]** Spread water over the sky area with your hand. You want it evenly moist, wet enough that it won't dry out instantly. Work quickly, streaking wet colors across the wet paper, starting at the top and working down. **[Use big brushes if you have them.]** The sky tends to be blue-purple at the top of the sky and goes to reddish oranges and pinks toward the bottom. You can't really control what the colors will do, but you can coax them in one direction or another by lifting the paper. It's best to work quickly and then leave it alone. If you have left some windows blank, put a little sky color in them.

**Alternative Method:** Paint the sky first, letting it cover the entire paper. If time and space permit, allow students to paint more than one, so they have a choice of which one to finish. Instead of coloring the scene, sketch it on black construction paper, cut it out, and glue it to the sky. Again, **shape** is the most important thing to consider.

CHARCOAL ON WET WATERCOLOR

# *Masks and Symmetry*

Grades 2–3

**Part I**

**Supplies:** 9" x 12" white drawing paper, soft lead pencils, scissors, black Sharpie permanent markers, (colored markers, and examples of border designs—page 37), copy of the mask drawing (page 37), images of tribes of the Northwest (Haida, Tsimshian, Tlingit, Chilcat), which may include masks, totem poles, paintings on hides and blankets—see book list starting on page 106; Robert Davidson, *Eagle of the Dawn,* edited by Ian M. Thom, University of Washington Press, if you can find it; *American Indian Design and Decoration*, by Leroy H. Appleton, Dover Publications, Inc.

NOTE: The art lesson should follow or be a part of a more in-depth study of Indians of the Northwest. If the students understand the meaning of totems, they will be better able to consider what kind of mask they want to make, what animal they might choose to represent.

**Motivation:** Write SYMMETRY on the board. Ask if anyone knows what *symmetry* means. No doubt there will be some confusion with the word *cemetery.* **Script:** We will look at some pictures of masks and totem poles made by tribes who live in Alaska and British Columbia. I'm going to give you some hints about *symmetry* and also *symmetrical,* which means anything that has symmetry. When you think you have an idea what either word means, raise your hand. **Masks are symmetrical** because **faces are symmetrical**, whether human, bird, or animal. Anybody want to guess yet? Okay, let's see if we can figure out what the masks have in common even though they are all different. [They have eyes and eyebrows, noses and mouths or beaks; they are painted; some of them have hair; the animal masks have ears. Talk about the mask drawing on page 37.] **Script:** This mask is **not** symmetrical. Besides the fact that it's a drawing, not a photograph, how else does it look different? [If they don't get it right away, cover the bottom of the mask and point out that the **top half** is symmetrical. Then cover the top half. Whoa! The nose and mouth are all lopsided.] **Script:** Are **YOU** symmetrical? Do you have two eyes, two hands, two feet? Two noses and two mouths? No, but the left halves and right halves are what? Yes, **matching**! Symmetry means matching—our left and right sides match. They are symmetrical. Today we're going to design a mask and make it symmetrical by using a simple folding trick.

**Demonstration:** Gather the class around you so everybody can see. Fold a sheet of paper in half, then open it. Ask for a volunteer to draw half a face shape. Put a dot near the top and bottom for the starting and ending points, and make a light guideline to show how close to the side the line should go. The line needs to curve out like the side of the face. Draw lightly at first, and when satisfied, go over the line, making it dark. Refold the paper and, using the scissor handle, rub over the line until it comes off on the other half of the paper. Retrace it so both sides match. Have someone draw one eye. Fold, rub, and retrace. Ask how many noses we need to draw. The first kid that says "half" gets to do it. Same with the mouth. Add ears or horns. Looking at photographs in the books for ideas, continue calling on volunteers to add face designs and decorations. Trace over all the lines with a black Sharpie permanent marker.

**Part II**

Talk with the children about the concept of *horror vacuii,* the fear of empty spaces. Some native cultures believe that evil spirits live in the empty spaces, which may explain their highly decorated baskets, pottery, weavings, and masks. Post the chart of border designs, but encourage children to come up with their own ideas of ways to fill the emptiness around the mask. These decorations should be drawn in pencil and retraced with black Sharpie permanent marker.

**Color:** This will not make you popular, but limit the number of colors allowed to **three**, plus black and white. Take another look at masks in the books, noticing the limited color schemes. The designs are bolder if color is controlled. Encourage children to think and plan ahead.

# Wilson A. Bentley...

Wilson A. Bentley (1865–1931) grew up in the small town of Jericho, Vermont. As a child he became fascinated with snowflakes. He even tried to draw them but was frustrated when they melted before he could finish. His boyhood passion became his life work as he discovered a way to capture snow crystals on film. His book *Snow Crystals* was published in 1931, and is now available from Dover Publications.

*Snowflake Bentley*, by Jacqueline Briggs Martin, is a delightful story of Bentley's childhood, brought to life through Mary Azarian's colorful illustrations.

# ...and Snowflake Variations

**Kindergarten**

**Supplies:** 8 ½" x 14" copier paper, cut in half (8 ½" x 7"), 7" tagboard circle patterns or Cool Whip lids, pencils, good scissors, several enlarged copies of snow flakes from *Snow Crystals*, posted where everyone can see

**Motivation:** (Have all the supplies at the students' seats, ready to go.) Gather the children around you and read or paraphrase the book *Snowflake Bentley*, then show them several pages of the Dover publication *Snow Crystals*. Tell them they should go to their seats and use the pattern to trace a circle and cut it out.

When you see that everyone has a circle, begin giving directions. **Script:** Fold your circle in half. What does this half-circle remind you of? A taco? [Draw a large taco shape on the board or easel, and put a "1" in it.] Let's remember it that way—first you fold a "taco." Now fold the taco in half. What does that remind you of (as you gently fan your face)? Let's call it a "fan." [Draw it and label it "2."] One more time, and this may be a little tricky, match up those two straight edges. [You'll have to help some children with this step.] Let's call this an "ice-cream cone" without any ice cream on top. [Draw and label "3."] How many times did we fold? Three! Taco, fan, and ice-cream cone.

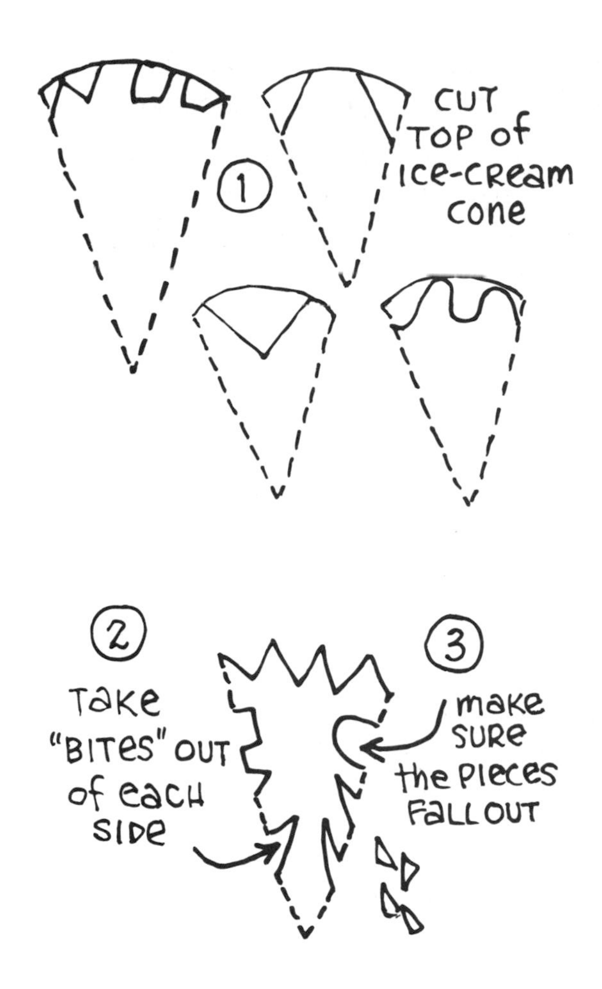

CUT
TOP of
Ice-CReam
cone
1
2
Take
"BITES" OUT
of each
SIDE
3
make
SURE
the Pieces
FaLL OUT

**Demonstration Script:** We folded three times. Now we will cut three different places. As you can see (referring to the examples on the board), the snowflakes are full of holes. As a matter of fact there are almost more holes than snow! See how raggedy the edges look? We are going to make some cuts, but don't unfold your snowflake until I tell you. The first thing we're going to do is cut the top of the ice-cream cone so it doesn't look so smooth. [As you demonstrate]. Cut off the corners, cut wiggles across the top, take "bites" out of it with your scissors. [Draw a couple of large ice-cream cones with variations of cuts across the top—label "1."] Now **you** try. Next we need to cut bites out of **both sides** of the ice-cream cone. You might take several bites. The pieces should fall on the table. If you just make cuts and nothing comes off, your snowflake will look more like a snow**ball**! What would happen if you hooked all your cuts together? Your snowflake might fall apart! [Draw a couple of diagrams showing different shapes of cuts—label "2."] Now **you** try. Do you see any snowflakes on the board that have holes in the middle? Do you have an idea how you could get a hole in the middle of *your* snowflake? [Take guesses.] There's only one place left that we haven't cut. Snip a little bit off the tip of the ice-cream cone if you want a hole in the middle. If you cut slant-wise instead of straight across, you might get a star in the middle!

Let the students cut more snowflakes on their own, reminding them to check your diagrams and remember "taco, fan, and ice cream cone."

LeT IT
SNOW!

## First Grade

**Supplies:** variety of colored tissue paper 4 ½" and 6" square, corresponding tagboard circle patterns, 9" x 12" or 12" x 18" white drawing paper, rubber cement or glue sticks, pencils, good scissors, and enlarged copies of snowflakes posted for all to see

**Motivation:** (Before you begin, pass out white drawing paper and circle patterns.) This lesson presumes that the students have already had some snowflake-cutting experience. If not, use the kindergarten lesson to warm up. With children gathered around, read or paraphrase *Snowflake Bentley* and look at a few pages of *Snow Crystals*, noticing the variety of shapes and patterns.

Have the students choose two small and two large pieces of tissue paper to take to their seats. After they all have traced and cut out at least one circle, review the procedure: fold three times (taco, fan, ice cream cone) and cut in three places (across the top, pieces out of both sides, and the tip if they choose). Tissue paper is a bit slippery. There will be some ruined snowflakes. Open gently! As children use up their first four pieces of paper, let them choose four more and continue cutting. (Hint: save time by tracing a circle on one piece of paper and placing another underneath before cutting.)

**Demonstration:** When most children have several snowflakes, show how to glue them to the paper. Whichever adhesive you're using, the procedure is the same.
**Script:** Brush (or rub) a circular patch of glue *on the white drawing paper*, about the size of the snowflake you're going to glue down. Lay the snowflake on the glue and gently smooth it down. How do snowflakes fall? [Use your hands to illustrate—first, with palms down and fingers spread, make straight, downward motions; then, wave arms and hands around randomly, wiggling fingers.] Snowflakes are fluttery. Think about that when you are placing them on your paper. Since we're using tissue paper, look what happens when I let my second snowflake overlap the first one. There's a new color! The snowflakes look like they fell through a rainbow.

Lay the papers out to dry. If there are some with a lot of empty space, crop off the extra paper before hanging.

**Grades 2–5**

Now it's time to fold circles in half, then in thirds to get the true hexagonal snowflake shape.

Experiment with larger circles up to 8" in diameter. Enlarge several snow crystals from Bentley's collection, fold them, and use as a guide for cutting.

**Stamped snowflakes:** Cut circles from colored copier or construction paper, 8"–12" in diameter. Fold as if you were going to cut a snowflake, then open, and flatten the circle by bending back on the fold lines. Using gadgets* (see pages 42–43), begin in the center by stamping one shape. Let the snowflake grow by stamping on each fold line (always think in sixes) or in the spaces between the folds. As the design grows outward, the spaces will get wider so that multiples of a stamp may be used to fill the space. This is a hands-on and visual math demonstration.

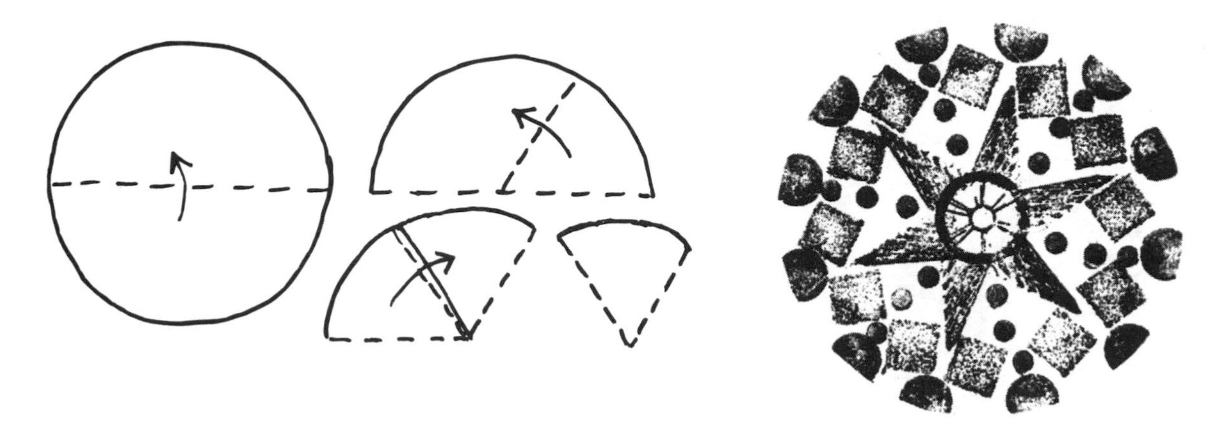

**Grades 4 and 5**

**Concentric Snowflakes:** Cut snowflakes from sturdy but "cuttable" paper, 5"–6" in diameter. Flatten by bending backward on the folds. Choose several shades of one color crayon and trace the snowflake repeatedly on white drawing paper (9" x 12" or bigger), working from dark to light or vice-versa. Trace around each hole and the outside edge before switching to the next color. Repeat this process with other colors, allowing the snowflakes to overlap and mingle or leaving space between them. This is a tedious process, which may only appeal to students with that sort of temperament. Variation: Use the same color family throughout.

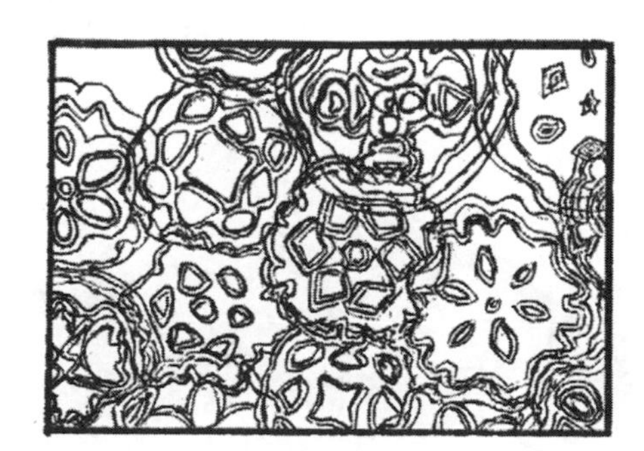

*For a simpler, less messy version, use markers, crayons, or a combination of the two, and *draw* shapes on the lines and in the spaces. You'll get better results if you brainstorm some possible shapes and designs on the board before you begin.

# Gadget Stamps

Grades K–5

**Artists Recycle!**

**Supplies: gadgets**—spools, small scraps of wood (including wedge-shaped pieces), parts of toys (wheels, for example), corks, plastic forks, old pencils (for the worn eraser ends), small lids, game pieces, interesting stuff you find in the street when you're out walking; **tempera paint** in five colors plus white; **damp paper towels or sponges**, soaked with paint and laid on **five Styrofoam plates**; variety of **leftover ends of paper**—great way to use up all those small but "too good to throw away" pieces. A variety of colors encourages experimentation. White print on black paper is striking. Gadget stamping works well as a whole-group or center activity.

**Organization: (for whole class)** Use six tables, or desks scooted together to form tables, one for each paint color. Place the gadgets and "stamp pads" on the plates. [To help identify which color is on each table, cut circles of construction paper (to match the paint colors) big enough to fill the center of each plate.] Put one plate on each table. Once the gadgets have been used, match them with the same color paint each time you use them. Of course they can be washed if you want to switch a color for a particular project. In general, there's no need to clean them up—life's too short! Plates and sponges can be reused. For easy access, all the supplies can be stored together in a plastic tub.

**Demonstration (lower elementary):** Put all of the plates and several pieces of paper in different colors and shapes on the floor on either side of you. Have students sit in a semi-circle around you. **Script:** [Hold up three or four gadgets and ask children to name them.] Ordinarily we would throw these things away. Artists see value in things that most people overlook. We're going to use these gadgets—most people's junk—to make art. [Select a long skinny paper.] What is a pattern? (Students are likely to answer: "A-B-A-B" or something similar.) Can you make a pattern with color (red-green-red-green)? How about with gadgets (spool-wood block-spool-wood block)? If I want to use blue paint with the spool and red paint with the wood block, how could I save time, instead of moving back and forth between tables? Right. Do all the blue spools first, leaving spaces for the wood blocks, then do all the red. [Demonstrate leaving spaces between the blue spools.]

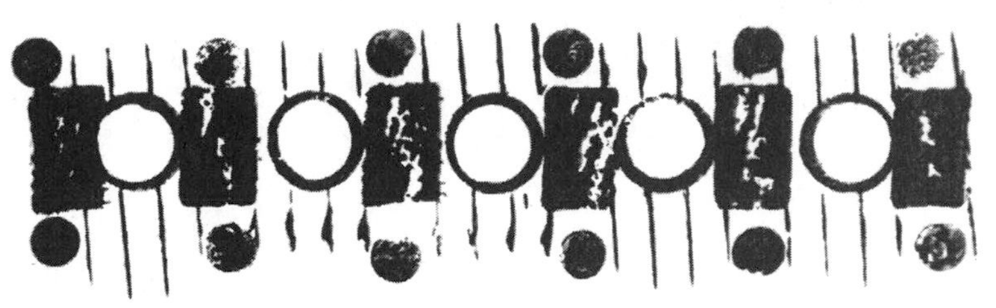

**Demonstration:** Stamp a round or square gadget in the center of a square paper. Stamp a wedge-shaped piece of wood at the top, bottom, and both sides of the center, then fill in between, using the same piece of wood. Continue building out from the center, asking students for color suggestions and which gadgets to use.

**Demonstration:** Make a picture of something—a wagon, train, boat, castle, person, animal, bird, funny face. Invite student suggestions for wheels, beaks, arms and legs, facial features, flower petals, tower roof…

**Bulletin board idea:** Hang gadget prints on a display about recycling or with math papers relating to patterns or symmetry.
Use gadget stamps to decorate folders or to make borders around pictures or writing assignments.

# Gadget Stamps

## Ideas for Upper Grades

**Borders:** Gadget stamps can be used as embellishment around the edges of artwork. For best results use only one or two so the border doesn't detract from the art.

**Radial Designs:** Fold a 12" square of drawing or construction paper in half as shown. Begin in the middle with a single, medium-sized gadget print. Build out from the middle, using each stamp eight times. Variation: Use one stamp for the diagonals and a second for the horizontals and verticals.

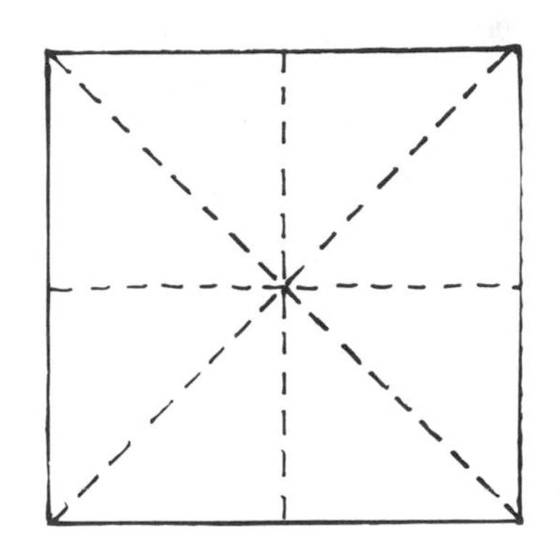

**Characters:** Invent cartoon characters, both human and animal, using only gadgets—no drawing.

**Invent:** Design an imaginary machine, vehicle, or building. Start small and add on.

# *Scissors, Shapes, and Glue*

Grades K–1

## Part I

**Supplies:** copier paper cut 4¼" x 5½" in three bright colors, a fourth color cut into 4¼" squares plus a fifth color cut into 2" squares, scissors, envelopes, glue, black copier or construction paper (8½" x 11" or 9" x 12")

This is a fun activity for kindergartners that teaches them how to look and listen, fold, cut, and glue. They won't even know that you're sneaking in some math skills at the same time. Do it in two sessions, and be ready to ham it up!

**Directions:** Have the children choose two of the three bright colors, one big square, and one little square. Give each child an envelope with his or her name on it.

**Script as you demonstrate:** Choose one rectangle. Hold it up, so I can see. Fold it in half. Open it up and **cut-cut-cut** on the line! Put one half in your envelope, and show me the other half. Fold it in half, open, and **cut-cut!** Put one half in your envelope, and show me the other half. Fold it in half, open, and **cut!** Put one half in your envelope, and show me the other half. Fold it in half and cut. **Put the two halves together**, fold them in half, open, and cut. How many postage stamp-sized rectangles do you have in your hand? Put **all** of them in your envelope!

Show me the **big** square! Fold it in half to make a triangle. Open and cut on the line. How many triangles do you have? Put one triangle in your envelope and show me the other one! Hold your triangle so it looks like the roof of a house.

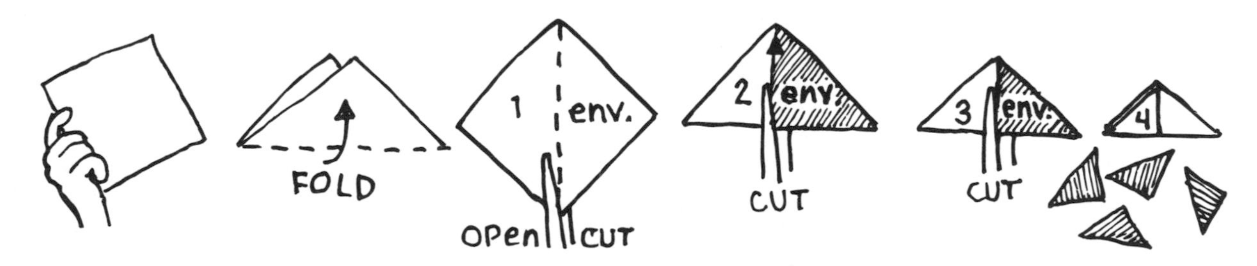


Start at the flat bottom, under the point of the roof and cut **right** through the point. How many triangles do you have? Put one in your envelope and show me the other one. Start at the flat bottom and cut through the rooftop. Put one triangle in your envelope and show me the other one. **Put the two triangles together** and cut. How many triangles do you have? Put **all** of them in your envelope.

 

Now show me the **small** square. [NOTE: have plenty of extras!] What shape do you think might be the hardest to cut without drawing it first? [Somebody will come up with "circle," but it may take a few tries.] I'm going to show you a way to cut a circle that makes it easier. Look at your square and notice that all four sides are the same, not long and short like a rectangle. A **circle** is the same all **around**. All you have to do is keep turning your square as you cut off the corners. It takes practice, so we'll try it a few times. **Watch!** You'll start with your scissors near a corner, but instead of cutting straight, **turn** the paper as you cut. [Demonstrate cutting out a whole circle, showing how you turn the paper as you cut around the corners. Some children will get it right away, while others will have to try over and over. Give them time to practice, and work with those who are getting frustrated. If some never get it, their more agile friends would be happy to share their pile of perfect circles!] When you have **two** good circles, put them in your envelope.

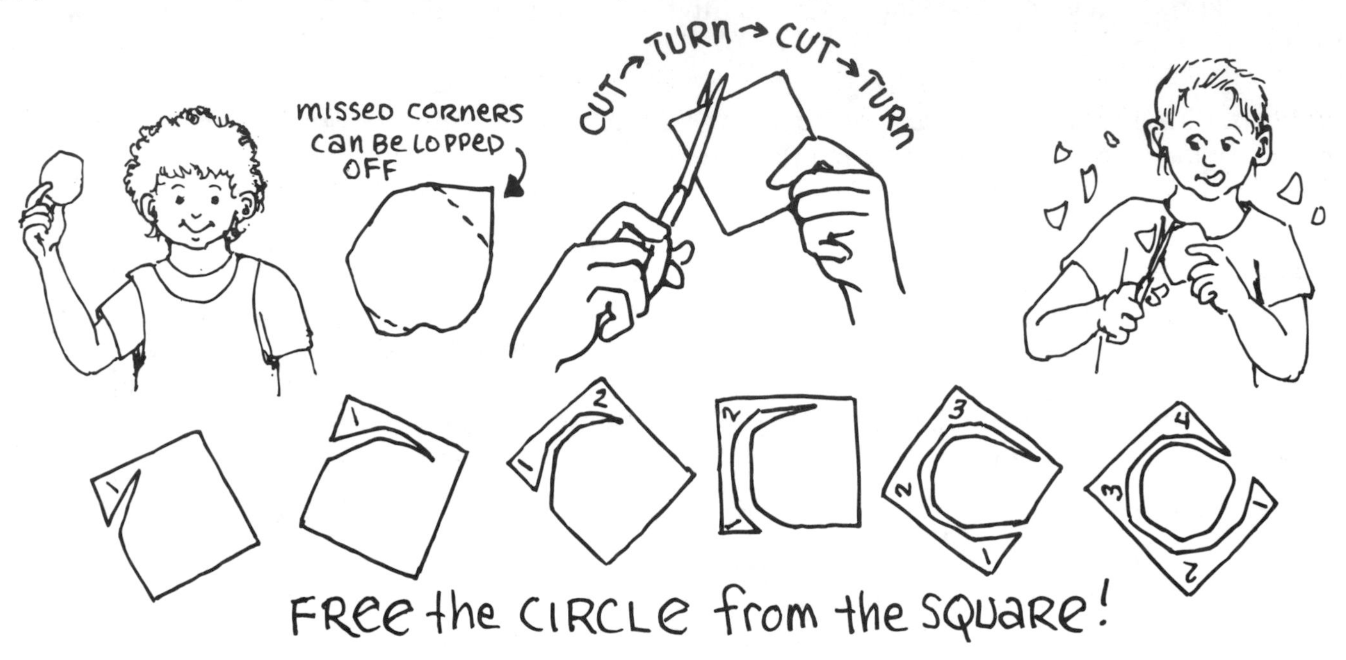
missed corners can be lopped off
CUT → TURN → CUT → TURN
FREE the CIRCLE from the SQUARE!

Choose a rectangle. You can hold it either way (vertically or horizontally). We're going to cut it into strips, starting at the bottom and going all the way to the top. When you have your rectangle cut into strips, put the best ones in your envelope.

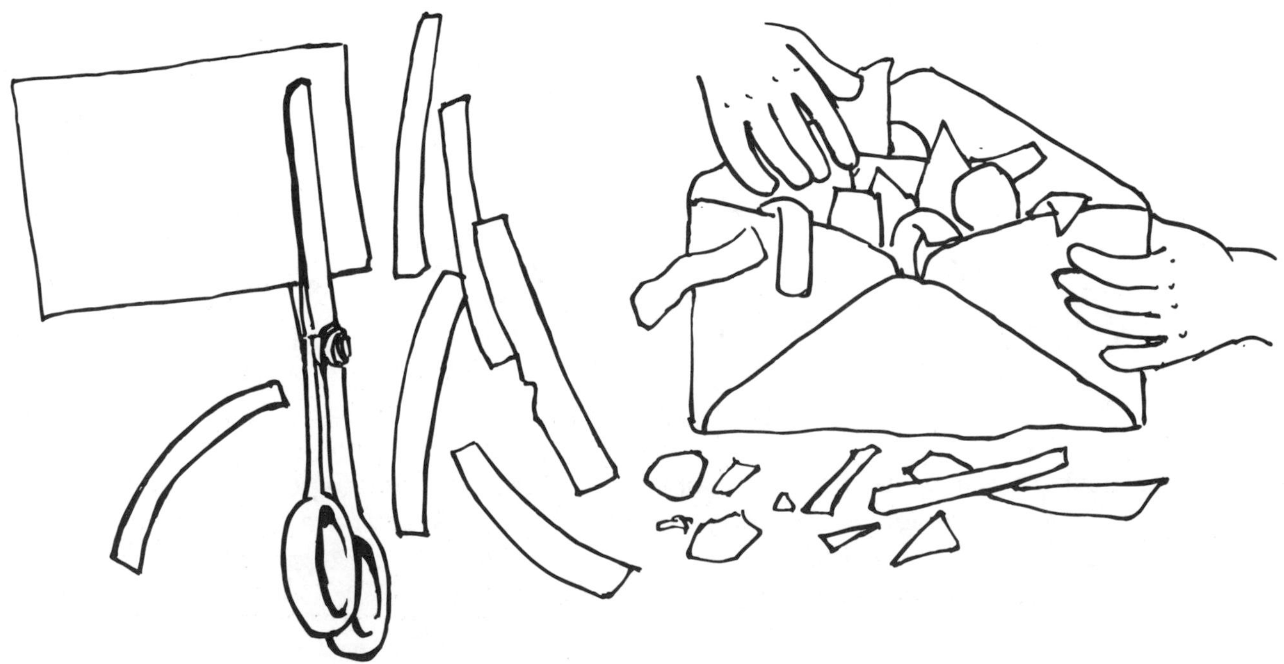

# *Scissors, Shapes, and Glue*

## Part II

**Supplies:** black or dark-colored construction paper 9" x 12", scissors, glue, extra colored papers from the first session (in case someone needs to cut more shapes), envelopes full of shapes, paper towels

**Directions:** Gather the children around you on the floor with a sheet of the 9" x 12" paper and your (or a student's) envelope full of shapes in front of you. Dump out the shapes. Put one of the larger rectangles on the dark paper.

**Script:** Could somebody add another shape to this rectangle to make a house? [If you're lucky somebody will pick a triangle for a roof—but other possibilities might be another rectangle for a door or a small rectangle for a window. For purposes of this script, we'll assume a triangle is chosen.] How does this blue (rectangle) door look on the blue house? Not great, huh? Why not? Oh, you can barely see it! Somebody pick a better color. These littlest rectangles might work for, uh… windows? Of course. Why didn't I think of that!?

DARK BACKGROUNDS
MAKE COLORS
LOOK BRIGHTER

[Dump the shapes off.] What other things could we make with our shapes? [Take suggestions and let a couple of students illustrate their ideas by picking out shapes and laying them on the paper. Here's one more thing that some children might want to try. Starting with a big or medium-sized shape right in the middle of your paper, build onto it, matching shapes as you go to make a **symmetrical design**. Another way is to skip the matching but thoughtfully arrange shapes in a **non-objective design**. See illustrations.]

JUST Ba-a-aRe-LY squeeze
ICK!
Leave some space between the GLUe Line & the eDGe of the paper

**Gluing demonstration:** Holding the glue bottle over one of the shapes, squeeze a generous glob right in the middle of it. Gingerly press this shape onto another shape and make a big deal about the glue oozing out all over the paper and your fingers. Wipe your fingers on a paper towel, then demonstrate how to touch the tip of the glue bottle to the paper and carefully draw a line a little in from the edge and following the shape of the paper all the way around. Although there are exceptions, most of the time the glue should be applied to the smaller piece of paper—the thing to be glued down. This seems like a no-brainer to mature people like ourselves, but many primary grade children like to estimate where the glue should go on the larger sheet, so that it will match up to the small shapes they hold in their hands. They can, with practice, get used to doing it the sensible way—but always have plenty of paper towels handy.

# Drawing the Figure

Lower Elementary

The first drawing of a person is typically a face, with arms and legs attached. By age four or five, most children will include a body, and with motivation, interesting details. Don't underestimate the effects of motivation.* Once a child has figured out how to make people (s)he will use the same formula every time. The "schema," as art educator Viktor Lowenfeld called this formula, is unique to each person, but one common thread is that parts of the drawing taken out of context, like dots for eyes, may mean nothing. (See page 3.) There are notable changes in figure drawings from kindergarten through third grade, especially if children are *encouraged* to draw people and motivated to observe the figure in action, where arms and legs are joined to the body, and clothing. By third grade, most children are drawing more naturalistic facial features, attempting proportion and movement (as in bent arms or running legs), and adding interesting details to clothing.

The first grade drawings at right were all drawn by the same student observing posed models. Notice the **schema**—eyes, nose, mouth, hands, feet, and legs. The first drawing shows the model holding an umbrella, which seems to be made of cellophane! This is the delightful art world of young children.

*In art instruction "motivation" has a slightly different connotation. It's more than just getting students to want to do the work, although that's part of it. Art motivation strives to call attention to a concept that challenges and encourages students to explore a new way of seeing or doing. Motivation can take a variety of forms, from physical movement to demonstrations of new media and techniques. Stories, (picture) books, music, and discussions about art and artists can all be used to motivate. Sometimes exciting school or world events are so powerful that it's worth postponing the spelling test to draw, while motivation is high, images and feelings fresh.

# Drawing the Figure

## Upper Elementary

Generally fourth and fifth graders want the people they draw to look "real." They draw hairdos, faces, and clothes with a concern for correctness. At this stage, the figures look real but not always natural. Compared to the drawings of younger children, upper elementary figures look stiff. Drawing from a model is a good experience from kindergarten on and especially in the upper grades. The possibilities are endless in relating costumed figures to history, sports, space exploration, super heroes, careers, fashion.

At this stage it is appropriate to talk about proportion in more detail. The body is about 7 ½ heads tall; when arms are down, the elbows are waist level; an open hand is not quite as big as a face. Use full-length magazine photos of people to study, measure (there's a math lesson hiding in here), and compare the relationships between body parts. To offset this activity, look at imaginative figure illustrations in books and comic strips.

Notice the individual styles (schemas) and the simple symbols used to indicate face and body parts in the early elementary figure drawings. These drawings were all part of a group mural of the playground. The boy with the large hands and prominent fingers was hanging from monkey bars. The girl with her arm extended may have been holding one end of a jump rope. Exaggerated body parts are a typical feature of lower elementary figure drawings. Notice the differences between the lower- and upper-grade figures. Older children pay more attention to hairstyles, clothes, and faces. Drawings at both levels are delightful in their own way.

# The Costumed Model

Grades K–5

**Rationale:** You may be wondering why you should attempt this activity. Here are some reasons: 1) It's relatively easy in terms of supplies—and not messy; 2) It forces students to make careful observations, like noticing how a hat fits on a head or the shape of a raised umbrella resting on the shoulder; 3) Overall it's an enjoyable experience for models and drawers; 4) Students especially enjoy seeing these drawings displayed, perhaps because of the close ties between classmates.

**Supplies:** 12" x 18" white drawing paper, pencils and erasers, sturdy table to use for a model stand, props—possibilities include hat or cap, scarf, vest, apron, chair, stuffed toy, broom, umbrella, suitcase, athletic equipment; clothing that represents a period in history or culture that you're studying; work clothes and tools. **Books:** *Norman Rockwell Illustrator*, by Christopher Finch, Courage Books, 2000; *Grant Wood An American Master Revealed*, writings by Grant Wood and others, 1995, Davenport Art Gallery, Davenport, IA.

**Room Arrangement:** Arrange tables or desks in a large semicircle, two deep, in front of the model stand. If you have access to drawing boards, shove the tables/desks aside, making a semicircle with the chairs. Kids will sit backwards on their chairs with their drawing boards resting on the seat backs.

**Artists/ Motivation:** Throughout history artists have used costumed models. Before students begin drawing, introduce them to artists Norman Rockwell and Grant Wood. Both artists used family, friends, and neighbors as models. Rockwell used people over and over again. If you look at a collection of his work, you will start to recognize certain people!

**Getting ready to draw:** Ask for a volunteer to model, and "dress" the person in some pieces of costuming. The model should sit or stand comfortably, holding something. Add a couple of props. After everyone is situated, prep the students as follows. **Script:** Drawing from observation takes concentration. Use your eyes. Spend some time looking carefully as you draw. The room will need to be quiet so you can focus all your attention on the drawing. Modeling may look easy, but it's not. The model will need to move a bit to relax a stiff arm or leg but will get back into the pose. Be patient. Don't criticize. Look for potential trouble spots—for example, the shape of an open umbrella over a shoulder looks different from an umbrella held overhead. Try to draw what you see.

Obviously, younger children should have shorter poses—5–10 minutes.
Fourth and fifth-graders can handle 20-minute poses.

# The Little Dancer

Figure Drawing for Kindergartners

**Supplies:** pencils and erasers, 9" x 12" (8½" x 11") white drawing or copier paper; *Degas and the Little Dancer*, Laurence Anholt; small tutu (check rummage sales or borrow), ribbon about 18" long, reproduction of Degas' *Little Fourteen-Year Old Dancer.* This picture would be an excellent addition to the classroom decor—find it at *www.artimages.com.*

**Room arrangement:** Arrange two rows of desks or tables in a semicircle with another table front and center for the model stand. Pass out pencils and paper.

**Motivation:** Gather the class around you (away from the tables) and read the story. Have the children take their seats, and choose a girl who is willing to pose as the ballerina. Try to find a child who isn't wearing a skirt or baggy pants. Ideally you're looking for somebody in tights, sweat pants, or bare legged. (The artists will have to transform her athletic shoes into ballet slippers!) Have the model (Sara) slip on the tutu, then tie the ribbon in a bow around her head or ponytail. Have her stand on the table and take the pose of the little dancer in the story. The children will enjoy the preparations and watching Sara position her arms and legs, with her head held up, just so. Talk to the class about what the model is doing. **Script:** How do her arms look? Can you see her hands? Look at her feet. Notice that there is a space between her feet. Her legs are not touching. You can figure out how to draw the arms and legs better if you draw the head, neck, and body shapes first. While we're drawing, Sara may have to move her arms and legs once in awhile. It's not easy to stand still for a long time. After she moves, she will get back in position.

**Demonstration:** Put up a paper where everyone can see and draw a head, neck, and body. Add the tutu, but keep it sketchy. The kids will come up with a variety of original tutus. Since they are spread out, the observers will see Sara from different angles. They should try to draw what they see from where they are sitting. The biggest problem is getting the arms around back.

This whole activity should take no more than thirty minutes. Give Sara some paper so she can draw herself when she has time. Add *Degas and the Little Dancer* to the classroom bookshelf.

# Uncle Willie's Story

Stylized Figures—Grades 4–5

**Supplies:** 12" x 18" white drawing or light-colored construction paper, yellow chalkboard chalk—can you find that any more?—erasers, crayons, black permanent markers and Sharpie permanent markers, watercolors (optional), book *Li'l Sis and Uncle Willie* by Gwen Everett.

**Background information:** William Johnson (1901–1970) grew up in Florence, South Carolina. He went to New York to study art and from there to Paris, Scandinavia, and North Africa. He returned to the United States at the beginning of WWII. Although he was an accomplished realist, he used a stylized approach to paint the scenes of African American life with which he grew up. Because he was black, museums would not exhibit his work. His paintings were found in disrepair after his death. They were restored and now hang in the National Museum of American Art in Washington D.C.

**Motivation:** Read, paraphrase, or just talk about the illustrations in *Li'l Sis and Uncle Willie*. (Although this is a picture book, some of the content is not appropriate for lower elementary.) Look again at these pages: title page, scary house, the collection of photos and paintings on a yellow background, and the collection of paintings on the last page. **Script:** When you consider all of the paintings, what differences in style do you notice? Can you think of any reason why some of Johnson's pictures look realistic? [Maybe he was trying out what he learned in art school.] What do you notice about the jitterbuggers? [Hands, feet, clothes—] Johnson exaggerated hands in several of the paintings. Do you think he made a mistake? Why would he make the hands so big? [Possible responses: In the jitterbug painting the dancers are using their hands to swing each other around. The children in New York show friendship by holding hands. In the river scene hands are used to baptize.] Johnson simplified his people on purpose to help explain who they were and how they lived.

**Assignment:** Draw a person or *type* of person (athlete, dancer, soldier, astronaut, relative) you admire, in the style of William Johnson. This assignment could be more specific to fit in with a unit of study. Possibilities: explorers or pioneers, professions, cultures, Black History month

**Demonstration I:** Tape a sheet of construction paper to the board. NOTE: you'll be drawing with chalk.* Pick a color that will allow students to see your marks. Draw a head shape and add the neck. **Script:** Start with a big enough head so that the feet will end up at the bottom of the paper. You may have noticed that people in Johnson's pictures have clothes, not bodies. The arms come out of sleeves and legs or feet from under dresses or pants. The person you draw may be holding something, wearing a hat, or moving. Think about how arms and legs in motion would bend.

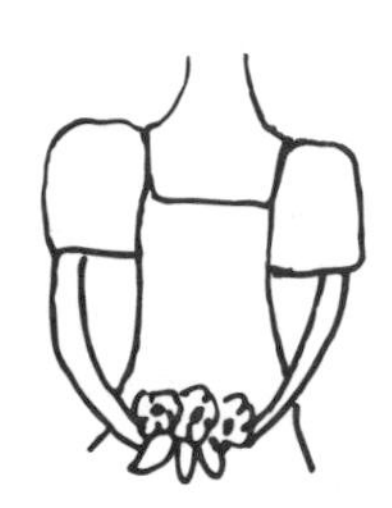

**Demonstration II:** When most of the drawings are done, call attention to your example. Demonstrate retracing chalk lines with the black markers, wiping the tips on scratch paper to clean off accumulated chalk dust. Color a section of your figure, demonstrating a solid application of crayon to cover the color of the paper. Take another look at the way Johnson used patterns in some of the clothing. Advise students to add a simple background design with crayon or watercolor if they so choose.

**Variation:** Retrace chalk lines with black crayon, **except** for patterns and details in the clothing. **Trace over the patterns with COLOR**, pressing down for good coverage. Using contrasting colors, paint over the patterned areas. Use crayon, watercolors, or a combination of both on the rest of the figure and clothes and background. Keep the background simple so it doesn't take the focus away from the figure. [see p. 14]

*Chalk doesn't permit the kind of detail you can get with pencil. The kids may not like the lack of control, but it teaches that art is more than photographic likenesses. Although it won't disappear completely, pencil erasers do work on chalk. Occasionally you find a child who has a physical aversion to the feel of chalk. In that case allow pencil.

# Historic Architecture

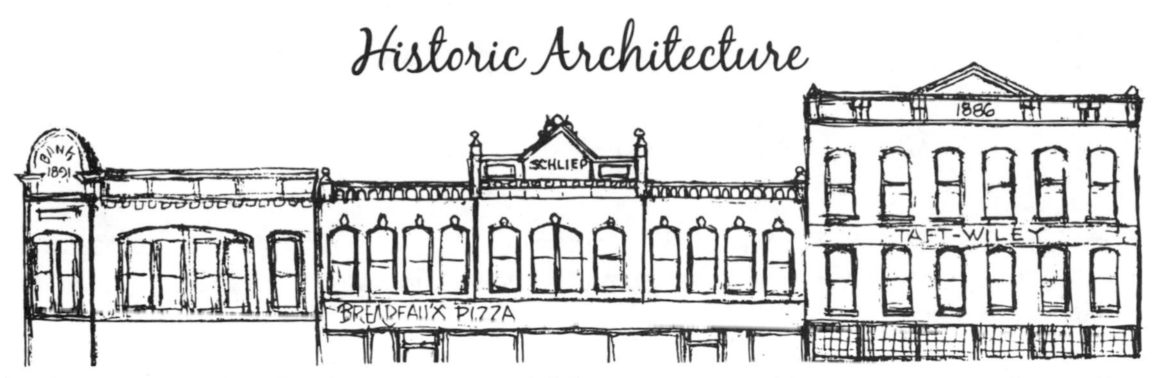


Can you recall a place you liked to hang out as a child? A restaurant, library, museum, theater? What kinds of memories are forming in the minds of our children?—day-care centers? fast-food restaurants? malls? video arcades? Many of their favorite spaces are part of huge modern complexes. Once you're inside, there's no sense of place. You could be anywhere! Because towns and cities grow over time, they have regional character. They have a history. Malls spring up all at once. Their appeal is bright lights, lots of merchandise, and a variety of stores, eateries, and entertainment under one roof. Some find it comforting that mega-malls are the same all over the country, right down to the anchor stores and everything in between.

Architecture is a major but often overlooked part of our history. Whether you live in a metropolis, city, or small town, you must be aware that historic buildings are becoming an endangered species*. If we hope to preserve what's left, we need to teach children to pay attention. Get to know the historic building enthusiasts and preservationists who live in your school district or community. Invite them to your class. If your Chamber of Commerce is affiliated with the Main Street Program, see what educational materials are available.

Architecture in general is frozen music. Friedrich von Schelling (1809),
*Oxford Dictionary of Quotations,* Third Edition, 1979

Man needs a serene architectural background to save his sanity in today's world. Minoru Yamasaki,
*Simpson's Contemporary Quotations, 1988*

Architecture is life, or at least it is life itself taking form and therefore it is the truest record of life as it was lived in the world yesterday, as it is lived today or ever will be lived.
Frank Lloyd Wright, *Ibid.*

Architecture is to make us know or remember who we are. Sir Jellico Geoffrey, *Ibid.*

*As an Iowan, I would include barns in this group.

 

# *Historic Buildings*

Grades 4–5

## Part I

The focus of this lesson is small-town Main Street storefronts. The ideas could be adapted to fit your own situation, with two goals in mind: 1) to develop understanding not only of the evolution of specific buildings, but also architectural trends, both good and bad, and 2) to introduce the idea of preservation.

**Supplies:** 12" x 18" newsprint practice paper, pencils and erasers, *optional*-straightedges—(rulers or poster board strips 1½" x 15"); books on American architecture, late-19th to early-20th century; enlarged copies of photographs of old commercial buildings from books (for educational purposes only); local publications on your historic district or downtown; calendar pictures

**Motivation:** If possible, invite a local preservationist, history buff, or somebody from the Chamber of Commerce to talk to the class before you begin the project.

Begin by asking the class to compare Main Street stores to shopping malls. Compile a list on a large sheet of paper labeled **Main St.———Both———Mall**. As students brainstorm, write the comments under the corresponding headings. Wait until ideas have run out before asking which place the kids like to shop. [Guess!] Now direct the discussion to your hometown shopping area (if one still exists). **Script:** Do you recognize or know the store owners? Do they know you? Why does that matter? How do you get to stores and restaurants in town? Do you ever ride your bike or walk? You walk from place to place in a mall but you have to get there first. It's likely too far away or too dangerous for a bike. As you're thinking about this, what is a *huge* difference between town and mall? It can be both positive and negative. [If they don't get it right away, give hints to lead them to the under-one-roof aspect of mall shopping. If it's already on the list, continue with questions.] Why is that a good thing? Why is it a bad thing? What do mall designers do to make you feel like you're outside? Is your town built around a square? What kinds of activities take place in or around a town square? Sometimes towns close a street for a parade or special celebration. What do you think would happen if nobody shopped in town? Have you noticed empty buildings? How do they look? Have you watched buildings being renovated? Why is that important?

**Draw-along:** Refer to the pictures you have posted as you describe, name, and draw the parts of an old building. The students should sketch along with you, keeping in mind that this is not the finished work. It's a way to learn facts about old buildings along with drawing tips and tricks that will make the final drawing easier. Don't worry about getting lines perfectly straight.

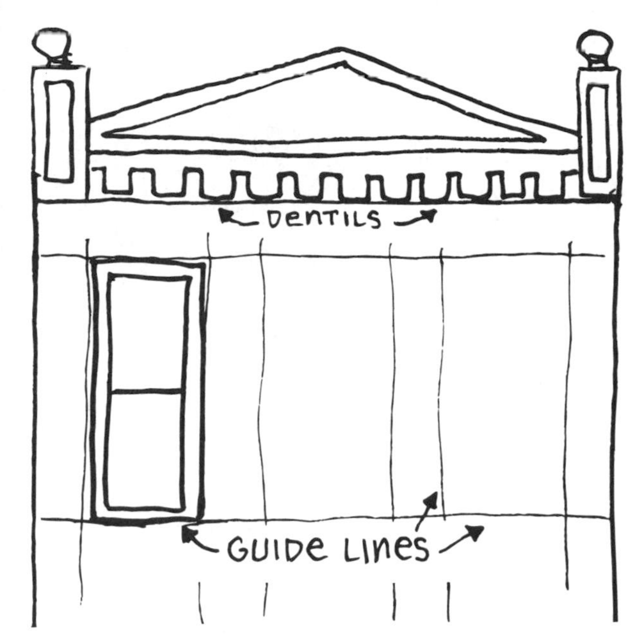


CORNICE
DENTILS ··· LOOK LIKE TEETH

Use the overhead projector and black Vis-a-Vis marker so that everyone can see. Begin by drawing the top half of the building, **cornice** and upper story windows. A cornice is a symmetrical decorative piece that may display the year the building was built and sometimes the name of the original owner. It also visually "lifts" the building. Cover up the cornice with a piece of paper, and notice the difference. Cornices are typically metal, painted multiple colors to show off the design.

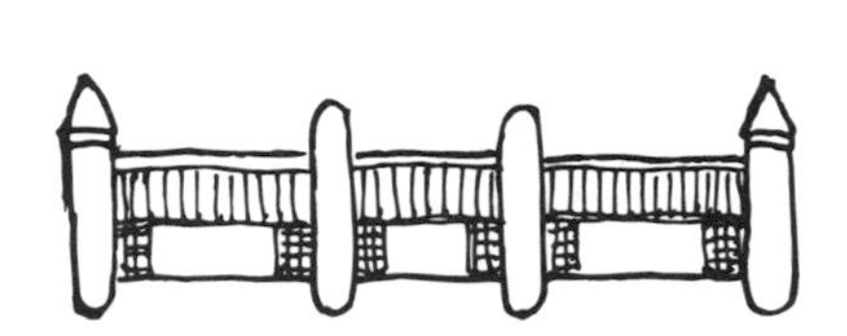

Small-town buildings are usually two or three stories, meaning one or two rows of windows at the top. Point out that the windows are evenly spaced and match each other. [Sometimes you find a double window in the middle of a row. Windows on three-story buildings may vary slightly between the second and third story.] Penciling in light guidelines makes drawing windows easier. Notice the decorative work above the windows. These **hood moldings** or **lintels** serve two purposes: to decorate and to deflect moisture from coming in.

The lower half of the building includes sign, awning, display windows, and entrance. You can now show your kids a couple of perspective "tricks" that will bump you up a notch in their esteem. Lead them through it, explaining the logic. **Script:** When you walk down the street, why does the sidewalk in the next block appear to get narrower*? [Because it's far away.] When you look at an awning or the indented entrance to a building, the same thing happens. Because the front part is closer to you than the back, the front end **looks** wider. Artists have figured out how to make a flat piece of paper look 3-D. You don't have to do this on your final drawing, but draw along with me now. [Follow the step-by-step instructions.]

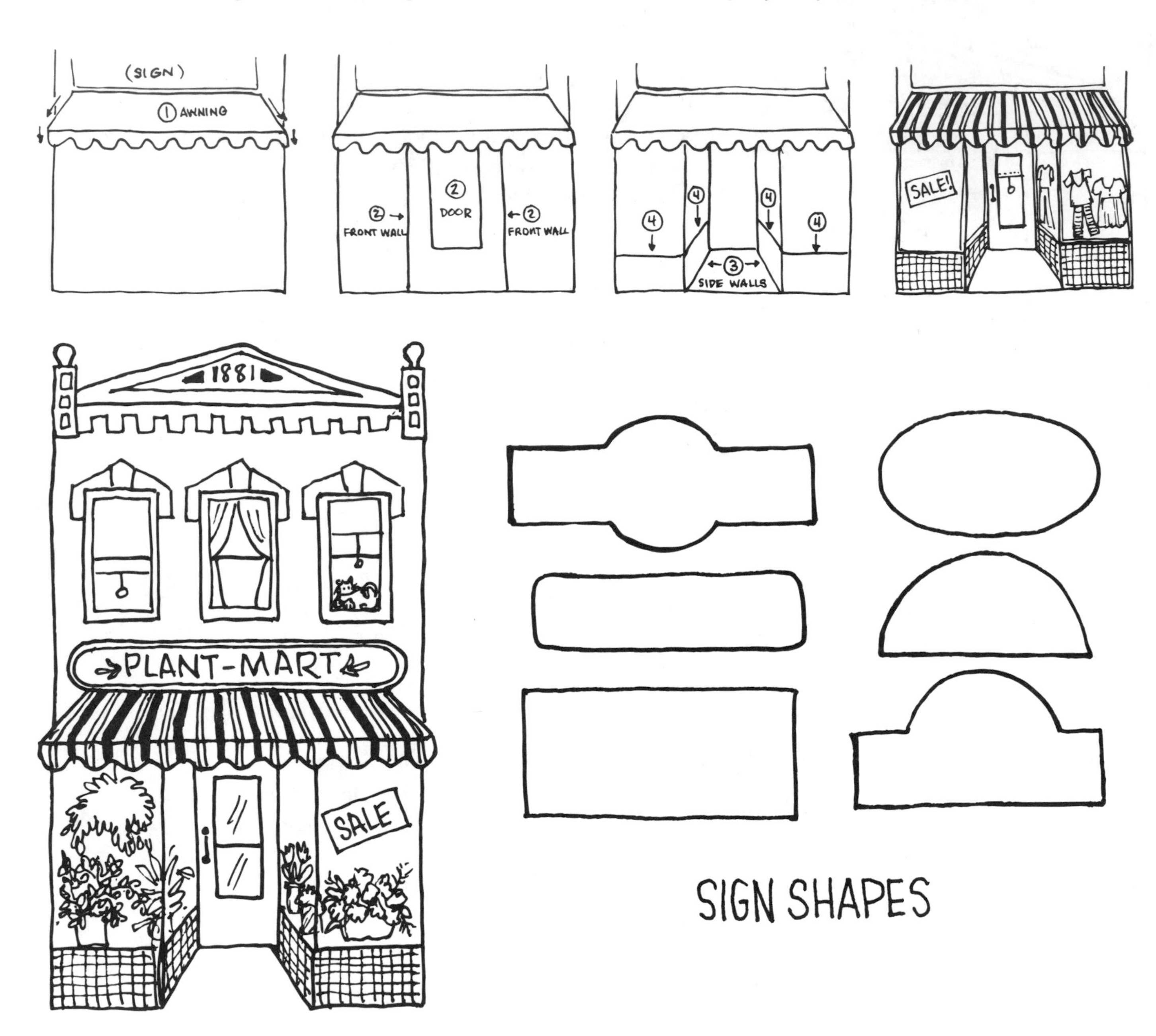


*If you don't believe it, try this. Next time you walk down the street, close one eye, and use your fingers to measure the sidewalk in the distance; then measure the sidewalk nearer to you.

# Main Street

## Historic Buildings— Part II

**Supplies:** everything you used in part one, except trade the newsprint for white drawing paper; sketches from Part I, straightedges. Choice of media for finishing may be black Sharpie permanent marker plus: crayon, watercolor, colored pencil, or a combination. Colored markers alone may be a little heavy but could be useful for accents.

[Pass out white drawing paper and the sketches from the first session.] Preface the discussion with the following directions: 1) the paper must be **vertical**, 2) because we go to a school which discourages substance abuse, and because your drawings will be on display, no bars, 3) now it's time for careful drawing, but **sketch lightly** at first so you can erase easily. After the sketching is done, use the straightedge to fix things up.

**Discussion:** Brainstorm types of stores that might be found in a downtown shopping area. List on the board. Some students may want to draw a "big box" building, because they don't get the concept that a brand-new store can be in an old building. I've had children upset because they wanted to draw a computer/video store. They protest, "There weren't any computers in the olden days!" Talk about a building in your area which illustrates that old buildings do indeed house modern businesses. The whole point of the lesson is to develop student awareness of historic architecture, so don't give in. **Script:** Refer to your sketches as you draw your building. Remember to draw lightly. The straightedge can help you get walls and windows upright. As you're drawing, start to imagine what kind of business you'd like to put in your building. It might help to look at the list on the board. What will the sign look like? How many windows on the upper level? What's up there? Apartments? Offices? Maybe the second floor of the same business? What is the building made of? What will you draw in the display windows? Don't forget the sidewalk! [Be sure to have all the visuals posted or on a table for borrowing.]

**Finishing:** There are several possibilities. For best results, give minimal choices: 1) detailed pencil drawing, using shading as well as lines; 2) retrace pencil lines with black Sharpie permanent marker—(X-tra Sharpie for small details)—and leave as a pen-and-ink; 3) retrace pencil with Sharpie permanent markers, then add color—crayons, colored pencils, watercolor

**Follow up:** Talk about local buildings in terms of the people who inhabited them. Ask students to interview parents and grandparents about particular buildings they remember: why were they important, how did they change over time, how were the upper floors used? Using this background material, have students write fictional histories of the buildings they drew.

 

# *Fancy Houses*

Grades 1–2

**Part I**

**Supplies:** 12" x 18" light-colored construction paper (pink, gray, lt. blue), yellow or white chalkboard chalk, erasers, black markers and Sharpie permanent markers, photocopies of Italianate and Queen Anne style houses, three of each (six different houses)

**Motivation/ Discussion:** Gather the class around you in front of an easel or white board where you have posted two house pictures, one Italianate and one Queen Anne. Ask students to *describe* (because they don't yet have the vocabulary to name) some of the things they see on the Queen Anne house [pointed roof, big porch, lots of windows, tower, steps, fancy decorations] and then the Italianate house [bricks, big door, tower, tall windows with round tops, flat roof, bay window]. **Script:** These houses are two different styles that were built over one hundred years ago. Those that were taken care of are still used today. We just described some of the differences we noticed. I'm going to show you some more houses and you decide which style they belong to. [As they decide, post the other four pictures near the style they're most like.]

The houses with pointed roofs are called **Queen Anne**, named for a Queen of England who lived a long time ago. Make your arms and hands look like a Queen Anne roof. That pointed, triangular shape is called a **gable**. There may be fancy decorations on the gable. The curved part with a roof that looks like a witch's hat is a **tower**. You can find lots of triangles on a Queen Anne house—and lots of windows—and big **porches**.

The houses that look like boxes, and have flat roofs and square towers, are called **Italianate**, because they were copied from farmhouses in Italy. The part that sticks out at the side is called a **bay window**. On the inside, the bay window is a good place to keep plants, because the sun shines in. Italianate houses often have a double front door with a window over the top called a **fan light**, because it's shaped like a fan. See those things hanging down under the roof? They are **bracket**s. It looks like they are holding up the roof, but they're really just decoration. Hold your arms straight out in front of you. Bend your elbows so your hands are up in the air. Now bend your hands backwards. Brackets!

**Assignment:** Draw a "fancy house." It can be like either style discussed or completely different, but it cannot be plain. Photos posted around the room will help students remember some of the details they might include. Encourage them to start simply and add on. Before they begin, each child should decide whether to have the paper horizontal or vertical. Draw with chalk first so corrections can be made easily. (Chalk also forces them to draw bigger.) When they are satisfied with their drawings they should trace over the chalk lines with the large black marker. [If the marker stops working, use a paper towel to wipe the chalk off the tip.] Most students should have no problem "building" and "adding on" to their houses. You can encourage slow starters by telling them to start with a plain, ordinary house, then add a tower, a big porch, windows and doors, etc.

## Part II

**Supplies:** everything from before except paper; crayons, piece of acetate big enough to cover 12" x 18" construction paper (two overhead sheets taped together); drawings from Part I

**Motivation/ Discussion:** Review the last discussion, and ask if anybody has noticed any Queen Anne or Italianate houses as they travel around town. **Script:** Today we'll think about two more things as we work on our drawings. First, when you look at the pictures, what do you notice around the houses? [Bushes, grass, trees, sidewalk] Second, what are the houses made of? [wood and brick] *Most* Queen Anne houses are made of wood, and *most* Italianate houses are made of brick. I have put a piece of acetate over Seth's drawing, so I can show you an easy way to make wood and bricks. Wood looks like straight lines going across the house—be careful to skip over the windows! [demonstrate] Now, if I wanted to change the wood to brick I would need to draw some lines going up and down. [On a sheet of paper draw example of wrong way.] Why does this not quite look like the bricks on our wall over there? Correct. For a strong wall bricks can't be stacked one right on top of another. If you've ever played with Legos you know you have to "stagger" the bricks. Here's an easy way to draw that. [Demonstrate staggered bricks.] Use the Sharpie permanent marker to draw details like bricks and wood and fancy decorations like brackets or the kinds of designs you see in the gables of Queen Anne houses. Add trees, bushes, grass, and flowers if you like. When you're done drawing, color your house. Since we're working on colored paper, press down on your crayons so the colors will show up better. It's not unusual to find many different colors on the old fancy houses around town.

**Variations:** Instead of drawing the houses, make them out of cut paper. 1) Cut the shapes of the parts and glue to background paper, or 2) Glue the shapes together then make a street of all the houses on a long sheet of paper. Draw and color sidewalks and trees on the paper. Draw, cut out, and glue on people, animals, streetlights, signs, etc.

# Castles

Grades 3–5

**Supplies:** 12" x 18" newsprint (for sketching), 12" x 18" white drawing paper, pencil, pictures of castles from calendars, photographs, and books, *Cathedral* and *Castle* by David Macaulay, regular and extra fine black Sharpie permanent markers, scratch paper, texture samples

Drawing teaches. Through drawing, children can experience other times and places. They can explore and wonder and dream in their drawings. This project is designed for that purpose. Your students will learn some pen-and-ink techniques as well.

TRY SHADING AROUND THE PORTCULLIS TO MAKE IT SHOW UP BETTER

TO MAKE THE DRAWBRIDGE LIE FLAT, MAKE IT WIDER (LONGER) AT THE BOTTOM

**Motivation:** Begin by looking at lots of pictures of castles and parts of castles. Discuss the unusual features the students notice—towers, arrow loops, portcullis. How? What? Why? Why were castle walls built thicker at the bottom?—(not only for strength, but also for ricocheting large rocks off them from above). What is an arrow loop—how did it work? What did the portcullis do? What would it have been like to live in a castle? Why were battlements needed? To help students understand what medieval life was like, read to them from the book *Castle* or better yet, if you can, show the **video** *Castle*, which features David Macaulay.

Before beginning the final drawing, have students make sketches on newsprint. This is the time to experiment, perhaps copying various features from the visuals you have posted or have made available. They might want to think of themselves as 12th-century royalty, planning a strong fortress to protect their subjects. After you give directions, students should sketch in their free time. The final drawing will begin with the whole group, using pencil on white drawing paper.

**Final Drawing Script:** Now is the time to think of the castle in a setting. *Some tips:* Don't put the castle at the very bottom of the paper. Allow a little space to invite the viewer into the picture. The main entrance is a good place to start. Draw a square or rectangle. Put a battlement on it. Draw a tower on the left or a colonnade on the right. Add towers *behind* the entrance. Draw the front door—would it look like your own front door? Use your sketches and the visuals to find ways to make your drawing interesting. Think about the setting. Is the castle near water, woods, mountains or hills? [Some will want to draw a battle. Tell students who are "stuck" to sketch on the newsprint to work out problems. Moat and drawbridge difficulties will arise. Do a demonstration as shown in the illustrations.]

Start simply…add on.

When the pencil drawings are finished, launch into the second part of the project, using black markers for texture and shading. (This may be a huge disappointment to students who have been planning a color scheme in their heads, but they'll get over it.) Compare this to icing on a cake. Textures and shading will make the drawings richer. Prepare several small sheets of paper showing various ways to shade. (See examples.) Look at the illustrations in Macaulay's books, noticing how he draws stone, bricks, clouds, water, wood. Learn from him. Give everyone some scratch paper to experiment on. After they have tried several ways of shading and practiced drawing textures they want to use, they should return to the castle drawings, first retracing all the pencil lines with marker, then proceeding to shading and drawing textures. Encourage experimentation with different point sizes. Variety in the size of the lines creates light and dark values. This is tedious work, but the results are stunning. If possible, let students work on their drawings for short periods of time over several days.

# Castle Vocabulary

| | |
|---|---|
| **motte** | **bailey** |
| **barbican** | **mason** |
| **crenel and merlon** | **undermining** |
| **curtain wall** | **arrow loop** |
| **drawbridge** | **murder hole** |
| **gatehouse** | **catapult** |
| **keep** | **sapping** |
| **moat** | **battering ram** |
| **steward** | **siege** |
| **portcullis** | **trebuchet** |
| **hoards** | **counterweight** |
| **garderobe** | **cesspit** |
| **turret** | **dungeon** |

## Extensions

Research the history of the children's song "Three Blind Mice."

Play a CD of medieval music while the class is drawing. They may object!

Find out what kinds of food people ate and have a medieval snack or lunch in the classroom.

Read stories about Robin Hood or King Arthur and the Knights of the Round Table.

Research the word *Camelot*. Why was it used to describe President Kennedy's time in office?

Play parts of the soundtrack from the musical *Camelot*.

# *Listen! and Draw a Gryphon*

Grades 3–5

This approach to drawing is useful for students who may doubt their drawing ability. It's fun, fairly non-threatening, and appeals to children's fascination with imaginary creatures. I've used this lesson with third graders. It could be modified for younger children. *The Book of Beasts*, edited by E.B. White, Dover Books, 1984, is an excellent resource, translated from the *Latin Bestiary*.

**Supplies:** pencil and eraser, 8 ½" x 5 ½" (or larger) copier paper

**Background information:** The *Latin Bestiary* was written in the twelfth century. It is filled with descriptions of animals, both real and imagined, their traits and behaviors. Gryphons have been found in the art of many different cultures. Descriptions and portrayals of the gryphon vary from culture to culture. The Tenniel illustration in *Alice In Wonderland* is one that many people identify with. Talk with students about the reasons mythical beasts might have come into being. How were our ancient ancestors different from people today? What kinds of fears might they have had? How did they get information?

**Directions:** After ascertaining that the students understand the make-believe nature of the gryphon, tell them you will describe it one feature at a time, giving possible variations of each feature. Since the gryphon is not a real animal, no one can criticize anybody's interpretation as they draw. Monitor as you proceed, going to the next feature when most are ready. It may take a little while at first, but students will soon relax and enjoy the challenge. Students *will* need their erasers. When they're all finished, allow time for comparing pictures. Collect and display!

**DESCRIPTION**—Pause after each sentence to give students time to draw.

The gryphon may have the back legs of a dog or lion. It may have a lion's front legs and paws or an eagle's front legs and claw-like feet. It may have the head of an eagle, with a curved beak or the head of a lion. It may have pointed ears or floppy ears. It has big, eagle-like wings. It has the tail of a lion or a serpent.

**FOLLOW -UP**

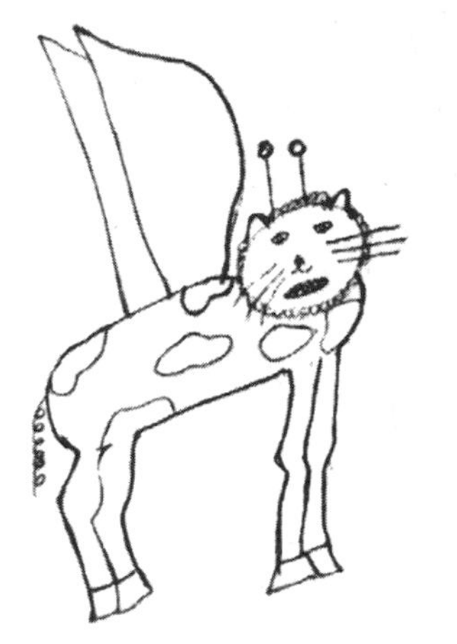

**Writing:** Have students: 1) write descriptions of their gryphons; 2) write stories about gryphons; 3) research and write about the history of and/or legends about gryphons.

**Art:** 1) Use the drawings as sketches for larger works in color, showing the gryphon in a fantasy landscape; 2) Work in teams to do mural-sized gryphons.

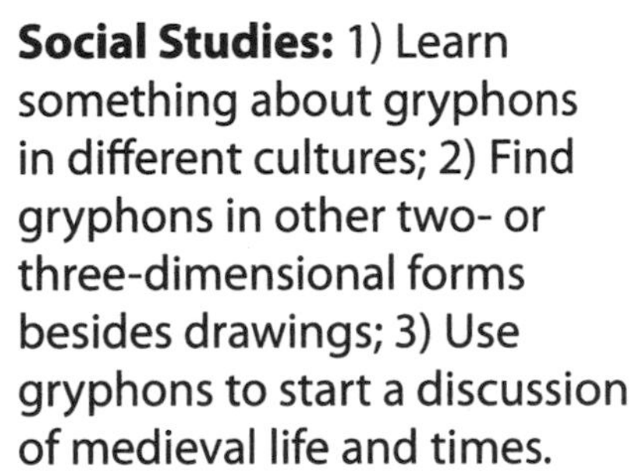

**Social Studies:** 1) Learn something about gryphons in different cultures; 2) Find gryphons in other two- or three-dimensional forms besides drawings; 3) Use gryphons to start a discussion of medieval life and times.

**BULLETIN BOARD**: Make photocopies of gryphons from reference books. Intersperse student drawings and writing with the copies.

# Masks

**Who wears masks?** The first things that come to mind might be tribal groups or kids dressed up for Halloween. Before you begin any mask project, brainstorm the subject. Also try to find pictures of masks from different countries and pictures of all kinds of people wearing all kinds of masks—doctors and nurses, football players, deep-sea divers, people with dyed or painted faces, people in gas masks, and people with beards and mustaches. It's surprising to discover how important masks are for a variety of people from a variety of cultures for a variety of reasons.

## Totem Poles

Grades 3–5

**Masks of the Northwest**

**Supplies:** 9" x 12" construction paper in several colors, scrap box, pencils, scissors, glue; pictures of totem poles and masks of the Northwest tribes, Haida, Chilcat, Tlingit, and others, diagrams of paper-folding techniques; if you can find it, *Robert Davidson, Eagle of the Dawn*, edited by Ian M.Thom, University of Washington Press, Seattle, 1993, an excellent resource about a working Haida artist/ carver, with beautiful color photos of his work (as of this writing, available at *amazon.com* and *alibris.com*); *American Indian Design & Decoration*, Leroy H. Appleton, Dover Publications, Inc., 1971; also see bibliography on page 105.

**Background Information:** Totem poles are a visual representation of a family or clan. Animal faces may represent mythological characters or, if given a human face, actual ancestors. Designs are passed down from one generation to another. To distinguish animals from humans, look for ears on top of the head. Bird totems have beaks, which may appear on a human face.

**Discussion/ Motivation:** Looking at examples of masks and totem poles by Northwest Indian tribes, list the animals you see. [Descriptions are found on the following page.] **Script:** A family totem is the indigenous (Native American) version of a family crest. The animal at the top of a totem pole identifies the family's clan. The other animals are taken from clan mythology or reflect real events in a family's history. Look at features that the totems have in common [eyes, eyebrows, ears, color scheme]. Animals that may be represented on a totem pole include the raven, eagle, hawk, frog, beaver, bear, wolf, dogfish, whale, and others. Each animal can be identified if you know what to look for. See next page.

**Demonstration: (Refer to diagrams.)** Show how to fold and cut a mask, with or without following a line. Experimenting on scrap paper helps students visualize how the cut shapes will look when opened up.

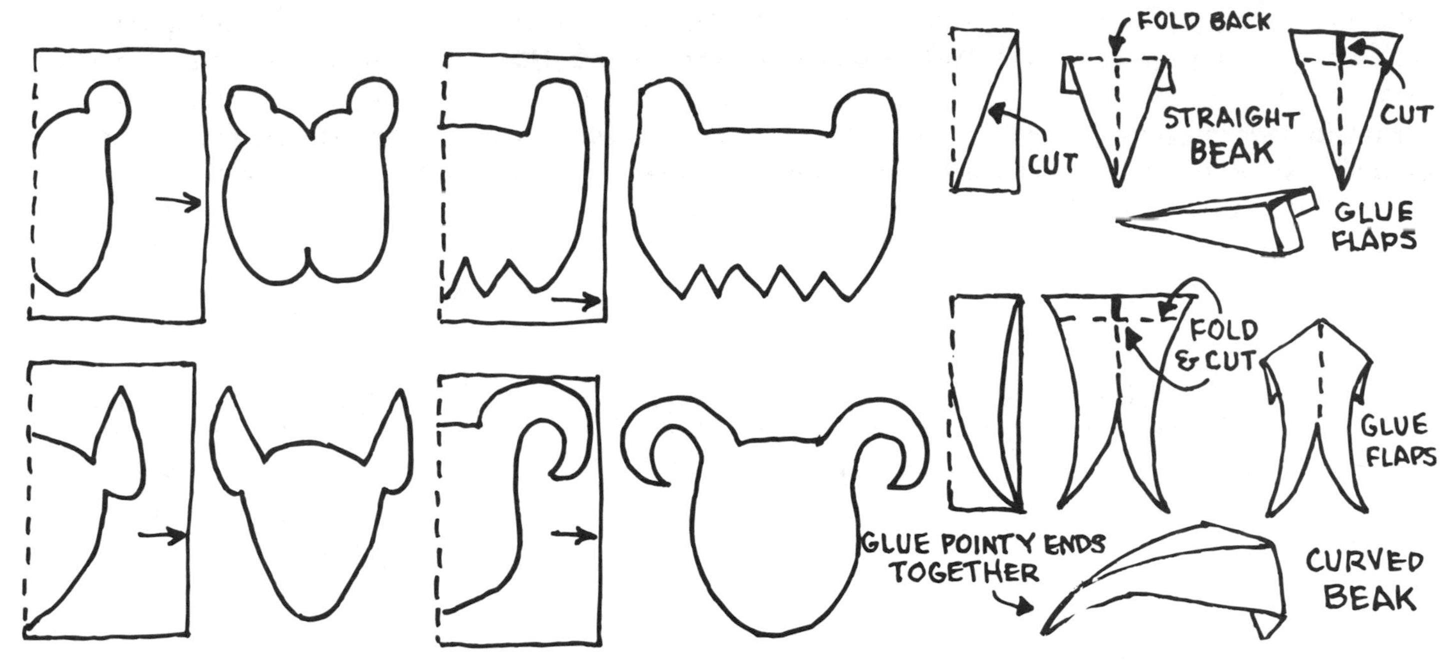


After students have selected paper and cut out the masks, they should choose three colors from the scrap box to add features. Make precut, paper strips (approx. ½" x 6") in different colors available to encourage their use as facial decoration as well as springs for "pop-out" features—p. 10.

Construct a totem pole in the room or hall, using bigger masks at the bottom and tapering to smaller at the top.

Have students write about the animals they chose to represent and why.

Bear—sticks out tongue, large nostrils
Beaver—big front teeth, holds a stick
Hawk—large, very curved beak
Eagle—gently curved beak
Raven—straight beak
Dogfish (shark)—pointed teeth
Killer Whale—large head with down-turned mouth
Frog—frog-shaped head, large mouth, bent front and hind legs, long toes

 

# Grandma Moses and the Rural Landscape

Grades 3–4

## New Insights for Maturing Students

**Supplies:** pencils, erasers, 12" x 18" white drawing paper plus whatever you choose to finish the work. Possibilities include crayon, black Sharpie permanent markers, watercolors, colored pencils or some combination. For discussion you will need one or two reproductions of Moses' works or a book including her work; for further motivation, display photos of rural scenes, farm animals, tractors and other farm equipment, plastic models of farm animals, toy tractors, etc.

**Background on Grandma Moses:** born on a farm in Greenwich, New York, 1860; liked to draw as a child; married at 21 to Robert Moses and had ten children; took up painting in the late 1920s; paintings of her childhood memories became popular and are to this day because they depict rural life of 19th-century America; died in 1961 at the age of 101. (Moses' landscapes would tie in nicely with Laura Ingalls Wilder's *Little House* series.)

**Discussion:** By third grade most children are eager to learn ways to make their drawings look "real." I have found that Grandma Moses' pictures appeal to students. Because her **landscapes** are filled with animals, people, fields, roads, machinery, and buildings, it's easy to get conversation going. The absence of modern farm equipment helps children understand how different farming looked over one hundred years ago. [The fact that Moses drew and painted from memory is important. Sometimes students who can't read or remember math facts have exceptional visual memory.] The discussion and art production would complement units on **geography, history, seasons,** and **rural life** in America.

**Art Motivation:** Begin by asking students to name what they see. Then ask someone to point to a building that looks close-up and someone to point to a building that looks far away. **Script:** The paper is *flat*, so the buildings you pointed out are really neither close or faraway. They just *look* that way. What **two** things did Grandma Moses do to show near and far?

[Pointing to the nearest building—then the farthest.] How did she make the one building look close-up and the other one far away? [The likely answer will be that she made one bigger and the other smaller. This is true, but that's only one part of the equation. The second part takes a bit more discrimination and may require some hints. Kids sometimes say that Grandma Moses made the smaller building "faraway."] Remember that the paper is flat! So what *else* did she do to show how faraway that small building is? It's up higher on the paper! Now this can be a problem if you think about the ground being on the bottom of the paper when you draw. Notice that Grandma Moses' pictures have very little sky compared to the ground. There *has* to be ground under the faraway hills or they will appear to be flying. Landscape artists call the layers of land *foreground, middle ground,* and *background.* [Pointing] What do you see in the foreground? Middle ground? Background?
**List:** Let students brainstorm things they could include in their landscapes and post the list for reference.

**Demonstration, Part I:** About third grade, many children have noticed and are interested in the three-dimensional drawing of two sides of an object. A demonstration of how it works is in order.

**Part II:** Let the children point to the different ground levels they see in the Moses painting. Layers are stacked on top of each other, and it looks perfectly reasonable. Upper elementary students are beginning to learn that it is possible and desirable to show the illusion of space in their landscape drawings. It can be confusing at first. The middle ground is important! It's the transition between near and far. Here are two ways to organize the space: 1) Lightly draw three lines to represent foreground, middle ground, and background. Ask students to suggest foreground objects, as you draw. Point out that the objects don't *have* to sit on the line. Continue, asking the class to offer suggestions for middle ground and background objects, and where they might look best. As in music and writing, "composition" is an important part of picture making.

 

2) Basically use the same procedure, but draw a couple of things in the foreground *before* drawing the middle ground line. This way you can allow the line to disappear behind some of the things you drew. This easy technique helps accentuate the illusion of distance.

NOTICE the DIFFERENCE BETWEEN the TWO APPROACHES

Unless you are taking a historical look at rural life in the late 1800s/early 1900s era, the students should draw what they know. If you are not in a rural area, use photos on calendars or in books for reference. The more visuals available, the richer the drawings will be. If you have models of farm animals and toy tractors, get them out! Borrow from another classroom if needed. [Because I live in Iowa, I've had no problem finding farm children willing to help their classmates with all kinds of farm implements and machinery.]

For best results, plan on two or three sessions, depending on the medium you are using. (See page 9.) You may want to have group motivation once or twice to remind the class about the earlier discussion or show them the next step if going beyond the pencil drawing. Children can then work on their own.

# Cut-Paper Still Life

Grades 4–5

**Supplies:** drape, large, medium, and small objects (interesting but not too complicated—teapot, whisk broom, stuffed animal, football, coffee mug—); scissors, glue, crayons, 12" x 18", 9" x 12", and 6" x 9" colored construction paper, variety of colors; print or picture in a book of Picasso's *Three Musicians*; chair on a table or your desk for still life set up.

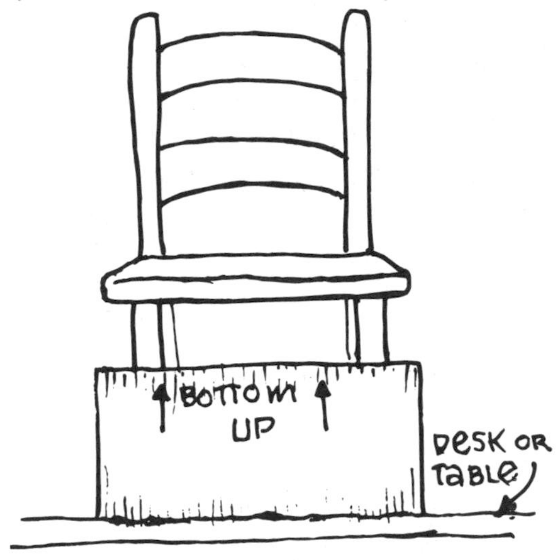


**Room arrangement:** desks or tables should be facing the still life, which is centered at the front of the room. To make sure everyone can see, you may need to put an overturned cardboard box in front of the chair to make objects at the front visible to students in the back row. Use a drape large enough to cover both—a plain, colored sheet, for instance.

Before you begin, let students go to the supply table and pick out paper, **two** 12" x 18" and one each of the smaller sizes. As the project progresses, some may want to exchange colors or use scrap paper for additional color.

**Script:** Today we're going to "build" a still life from back to front, using cut paper rather than pencil. (groans) How do you think this process will affect the way your pictures will look? [Possible answers: they'll look stupid, ugly; more colorful; not as much detail, plain shapes] Look at this painting of *Three Musicians* by Picasso. It's not "realistic," but we can identify three characters and musical instruments. Why? [from the shapes]. Exactly! I'm going to put this (physical) still life together one piece at a time, starting with the backdrop or drape. Each time I add something you'll cut out the shape you see, either free-hand or lightly outlined in pencil first, then cut out. [Arrange the drape over the chair (and box).] The drape will be the biggest shape. Although it would be a rectangle if hanging on a clothesline, pay attention to the shape it makes as it flows over the chair. Notice how it's narrower at the top and wider at the bottom. Use your paper vertically. Choose one of the two large sheets of paper for the background and use the other one for the drape. **Think big**—the drape should touch at least three edges of your background. . [This probably won't happen in many cases, but say it anyway.] **Think artistically**—don't worry about making it exactly the shape you see. After you have cut it out, glue it to the background. [Allow time for work, then proceed.]

**HINT:** It would be wise to set up the whole still life when there are no children around, so you can have in mind how you want to place the objects, **before** doing it in front of the class. Check it from different angles in the room. If you're like me, you'll probably try several times before hitting on the best arrangement.

Place the first object on the drape. If objects are more than one color, let students use their smaller pieces of paper, scrap box paper, or scraps traded with their classmates for the needed colors. Use crayons to draw patterns—stripes, spots, checks, etc.

Each time you add an object, talk about size and shape. Students should take a moment to look carefully before they cut. To keep things moving, postpone gluing each piece to the background until all the pieces are cut.

add the chair if you want....

If the still life is on a table and out of the way, this project could be done in small time slots over several days.

  

# *Stuffed Toy Still Life*

Grades 1–3

**Supplies:** Assortment of stuffed animals and rag dolls, perhaps solicited from class members; 12" x 18" white drawing paper, pencils and erasers, black Sharpie permanent markers, crayons, watercolors; borrow drawing boards from the art room if possible

**Room arrangement:** Move the furniture aside, except for chairs for each animal; these should be evenly spaced around the room. The children will sit on the floor.

**Discussion / Demonstration*:** Gather the class at the white board and have a couple of animals sitting on one of the desks or tables that have been moved. Two varieties of bears would be good for the sake of comparison. Tell the students that they will be looking closely at the animals, trying to draw exactly what they see. **Script:** I am going to draw this bear. I will purposely make some mistakes. See if you can figure out what's wrong. [Refer to the illustrations for the kinds of mistakes you might make. Astute kids may also find mistakes you didn't intend. That's a good thing! It means they're looking carefully. As someone identifies an error, ask how it could be fixed.] Oh, I see. (Teddy's feet turn out—the bottoms of the feet are oval, not round.) There. Does that look more like it? As you draw, look carefully and try not to make anything up. Use little tricks. For instance, when you're drawing the animals' ears, look and see if they're right above the eyes or off to the side a little. Some things may be hard to figure out. Take time to look, then do the best you can.

POT-BELLY'S HEAD & BODY ARE ABOUT THE SAME SIZE
THE ARMS APPEAR TO BE JOINED TO THE HEAD... THE PAWS TOUCH THE KNEES
OLD TEDDY BEAR
BEAR'S HEAD IS TILTED...THE EYES TOUCH THE MUZZLE. THE ARMS CURVE...THE FEET TURN OUT... SOLES ARE EGG-SHAPED
RAG DOLL
BIG BUTTON EYES!
DOLL IS MORE INTERESTING WITH ARMS & LEGS CROSSED
...PIG TAILS HANG DOWN


*If you're not too sure of your drawing skills, practice before you demonstrate in front of the class.

**Procedure:** Children may choose which animals they want to draw and move from place to place as they finish an animal. Remind them to be respectful of one another if several people are grouped around one animal. They may organize the drawing however they like. Some may create a toy shelf with the animals (and dolls) lined up in a row. Some may put them in some other setting or no setting at all. When they are finished with the drawings, they should trace over the lines with a black Sharpie permanent marker. They can stop there or continue with crayons. A final step might be to wet the paper and use a large, soft brush to paint a watercolor background. Wetting the paper helps the color flow and keeps it from getting too dark. (See page 14.)

# *Fun With Lines*

Grades K–2

**Supplies:** 12" x 18" newsprint, two to three sheets per child; black Sharpie permanent markers, regular black markers (bigger tips); something to protect desks or tables from marker "bleed"; *Lines, Spines, and Porcupines* by Anne Samson (check *bookfinder.com*) or *Harold and the Purple Crayon* by Crockett Johnson; photocopies of line drawings from art history and children's books (Suggestions: David Macaulay's *Castle* or *Cathedral*, Tana Hoban's *Spirals, Curves, Fanshapes, & Lines*; *Family Walk*, drawing by Paul Klee; *The Hostess*, wire sculpture by Alexander Calder; comic strip characters). Post where children can see.

**Motivation/ Procedure:** Read the book and look at the illustrations. Call on students to point out lines they see in the classroom. (If the weather is nice, you could go out to the playground and do the same thing.) Have the children "line" up very close together, then while leading them in a curving, loopy sort of path, have them observe their human line. (They have to pay attention and stay tight.) Finally, lead them in a snail-shell spiral, and as they are giggling, reverse and lead them out again. Staying in line, march them back to their seats, having them drop off when they reach their own places.

**Draw-along:** With papers vertical and using the larger markers, have the class practice drawing different kinds of lines. [See illustrations.] Make sure there is plenty of extra paper available. Switch to the Sharpie permanent markers, noticing the difference in the thickness of the lines.

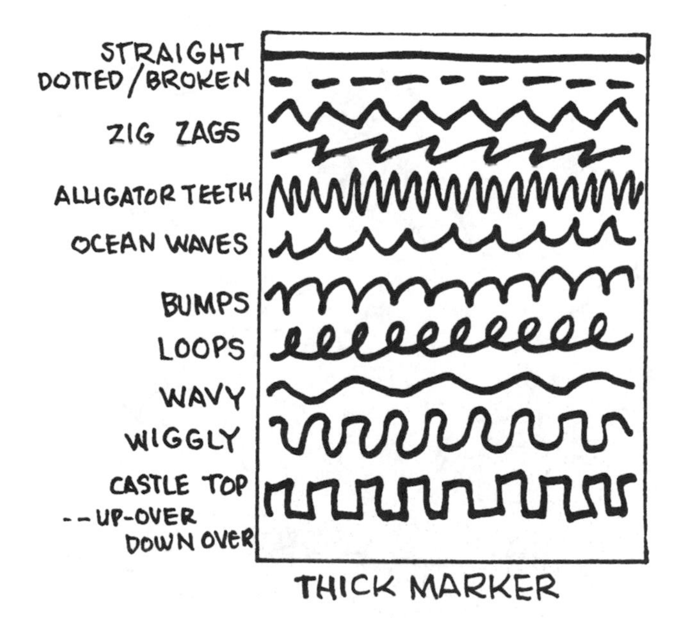


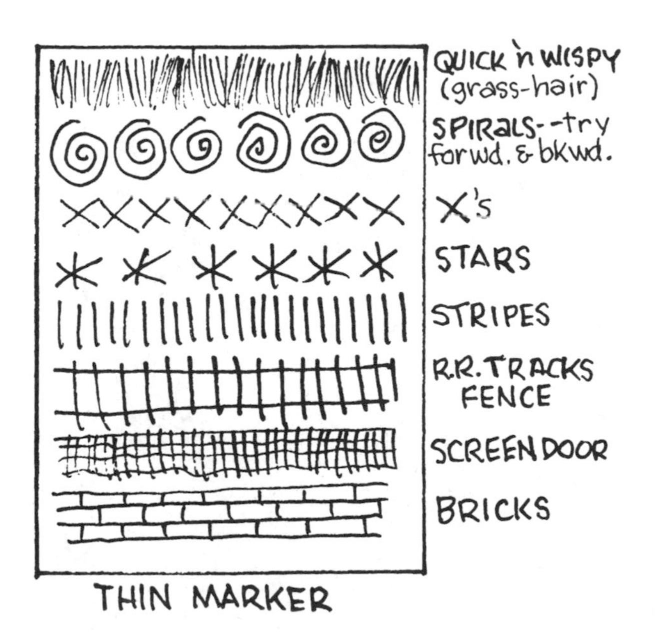

**Script:** We've practiced making different kinds of lines, using both thick and thin markers. You can look at the examples on the wall to see how different artists use lines to make art. Now it's your turn to make a line drawing. You can make whatever you like. You have two markers, one thin, one thick. Think how you will use each one. For instance, if you were going to draw a big, ugly monster, which marker would you use? Yes, the big one, because it would make the monster's body look strong and scary. Now, what if you wanted to give the monster sharp teeth and toenails and make it hairy all over? Right! Switch to the thin marker. Here's another example: Castle? and bricks? How about a **big** tree? tiny branches, bark and leaves? Use the right tool for the job. Experiment with thin and thick lines. Be sure you sign all of your papers. I will choose one from everybody to hang on the bulletin board, and you may take the rest home.

# Fun With Shapes

Grades 1–2

**Supplies:** construction paper: 12" x 18" black, and 6" x 9" red, yellow, and blue; glue, scissors, and paper towels; **flannel board** (remember that old low-tech device?) and several sizes of flannel circles, squares, triangles, and rectangles in each color. NOTE: The triangles and rectangles should also be of various dimensions.

The motivation for this activity could be one of the many books about shape which are available in children's bookstores and libraries. Try to find one that is limited to the simple shapes—circles, squares, triangles, and rectangles. My favorite is the out-of-print *Squares Are Not Bad* by Violet Salazar. Copies can be found on internet sites (*alibris.com, biblio.com*, and *bookfinder.com)*, but they are pricey. Whatever book you use, or even if you just have a conversation about shapes, you are setting the stage for the project.

Pass out paper, one each of black, red, yellow, and blue, and have children get out their glue and scissors before you begin.

Gather the class around you on the floor to read the book. Have the flannel board with small groups of each shape on it, propped up where everyone can see. Explain that these are the only shapes allowed today. Placing a square in the middle, ask for a volunteer to make a house by adding a roof shape. Let others take turns adding things. Talk about color. Put a door on the house the same color as the house. "What's wrong with this?" [The door doesn't show up.] Take the house apart and ask, "What else can we make with these shapes?" Call on someone to make another "shape picture." **Script:** You can make whatever you like, but use **only** squares, rectangles, triangles, and circles. There are many possibilities for pictures using these simple shapes. Look around the room, taking turns naming circles, squares, triangles, and rectangles, standing alone or as part of something else. If you need more than one of a shape, how can you save time? Right, put 2 or 3 layers of paper together and cut them all at once. [Demonstrate]

Encourage the children to think for themselves. Some may make a design or one large image, while others might create a shape narrative. Remind them of **THE RULES:** cut **only circles, squares, triangles, and rectangles**; put the shapes together to make something. Review good gluing habits (page 48) and send students back to their seats to work.

If some shape pictures don't fill the paper, crop before hanging.

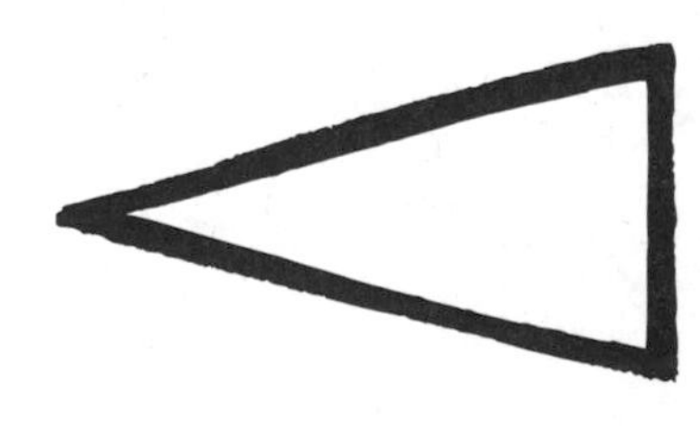

# Cooperative Shapes

Grades 2–3

Here's an activity that promotes working as individuals for the good of the group. Teamwork without arguments!

**Supplies:** scissors, copier or construction paper in several bright colors, 5 ½" x 8 ½" (6" x 9"); black or dark colored construction paper, 12" x 18", glue (HINT: Don't let the glue come out until the students have had time to experiment.)

**Preparation:** Have each child choose three of the bright colors, then have them count off by sixes. All ones will cut circles; twos, squares; threes, triangles; fours, rectangles; fives, diamonds, and sixes, crescents. Students should cut small, medium, and large versions of their shapes. They may want to cut the center out of some. The triangle, rectangle, and diamond groups should cut different varieties of those shapes. Let them go back for more paper, one or two sheets at a time. Have the groups put their shapes in six separate shallow containers—clean pizza boxes would work well—or on separate counters in the room. Students will need room to rummage through the shapes. (If you only have a short period of time, stop at this point and store the shapes in separate folders until you are ready for the next step.)

**Procedure:** Each child should choose five pieces from the shape piles—if some choose all one shape, it's okay, but no more than five to start—and one sheet of the 12" x 18" construction paper.

**Script:** Play around with your shapes, arranging and rearranging until an idea comes to you. You might see an object or maybe the beginning of a nice design. When you have an idea, get four or five more shapes and keep adding. Except for small changes, try to leave the shapes as they were cut. When you are ready to glue, pick up one piece at a time and carefully glue it down. (See tips on gluing, page 48.) Add more shapes if you need them.

**Evaluation/Conversation:** What's the point of making and using the piles of shapes instead of thinking about what you want to make and then cutting all the shapes yourself? How did working like this change the way you thought about what to make? How did it change the way your picture looks? The thought process was different. Rather than starting with an idea and figuring out what shapes you needed, you had to work backwards, taking the shapes and figuring out what they could become. The shapes helped you decide what to make. Your finished art has a different look because you couldn't have made these particular art works without everybody's help. How do you feel when you see the shapes you cut out in your classmates' artworks?

**Tip:** If some of the finished pieces don't fill the paper, crop the paper to make it fit the art.

# Sadie, Sadie the Pattern Lady

Grades 1–2

**Supplies:** 12" x 18" white drawing paper, felt tipped markers in assorted colors and tip sizes

When I started teaching, mention "patterns" and most young children thought of wallpaper. Today when you ask about patterns, you're likely to get a mathematical response, such as "one-two, one-two," or they will say, "It's something you trace around." This activity encourages students to think about and use patterns in their artwork. Before you get into the motivation, explain that "pattern" can refer to repeated lines and shapes. Repeated lines are called "stripes." Ask students what repeated circles are called (polka-dots). Have them look around the room and at one another's clothing to find and name other patterns.

**Motivation:** Tell the class to listen carefully as you read "Sadie-Sadie, the Pattern Lady," because you will ask them questions about it to see what they remember.

Sadie-Sadie, the pattern lady,
Is the prettiest lady in town.
She ties ribbons fair in her patterned hair,
And has flowers all over her gown.
She takes her socks from a polka-dot box;
She puts them on pretty plaid feet.
Her beautiful shoes are a number of hues
That flash as she walks down the street.
Her favorite bonnet has feathers upon it
And sashes that tie 'neath her chin
Her apron is darted and multiple-hearted.
It fastens in back with a pin.
And when people meet her, they happily greet her.
She glows from her toes to her crown.
Yes, Sadie-Sadie, the pattern lady,
Is the prettiest lady in town.

Explain any words the children might not have understood, then quiz them. What did Sadie wear in her hair? What did her apron have on it? What did her feet look like? What was on her bonnet? And so on. Then introduce Dashing Dan, Sadie's boyfriend, and remind everyone to listen.

Dashing Dan is a pattern man.
He comes from a place called Patternland.
He wears a checked coat and a tall striped hat
When he goes for a stroll with his calico cat.
His pants, a spectacular sight to behold,
Are covered with patterns of purple and gold.
A bright, shiny buckle on each shiny boot
Reflects the designs of his big bumbershoot.*
His favorite tie was a gift from his mother.
It's dotted and spotted unlike any other.
And the colorful garment that covers his chest
Is a beautiful, sparkling, polka-dot vest.
So if you fancy colors of pink, green, and blue,
I'll tell you a secret, between me and you,
That Dashing Dan is the handsomest man
Who lives in the village of Patternland.

Again, explain any difficult words, then quiz the students. Tell them they should draw Sadie or Dan (or both), but they needn't draw them exactly as described. The important thing is to use lots of patterns. Encourage students to work big, beginning with a grapefruit-sized head so that the feet will reach the bottom of the paper. As they draw, comment on their work. "I see Joey has drawn Dan's umbrella. Good, Erin! Sadie's bonnet looks pretty with all those feathers." Your remarks will keep everyone thinking. Encourage the kids to draw ground, sky, trees, and flowers along with the people. These things may look different in Patternland. Toward the end of the session, reread the poems to inspire last-minute additions.

*British word for "umbrella"

# Matisse, the Cutting Edge

Grades 3–4

## Part I

**Supplies:** fadeless or colored copier paper—variety of colors cut into 3" x 4 ½" pieces, laid out on a counter or table; scissors; envelope for each child to keep shapes in

**Background information:** Henri Matisse (1869–1954) was a French painter who, because of illness in his later life, turned to cut paper, a medium which allowed him to work from a bed or wheelchair. Assistants painted large sheets of paper in flat colors, which he would then cut, using his scissors as a drawing tool. Some of his cutouts are wall-sized and were assembled by assistants under his direction. *Jazz*, a book Matisse produced in the 1940s, is illustrated with cutouts. *Henri Matisse: Jazz* (Pegasus Library) is available inexpensively on *amazon.com*—used books.

The idea of drawing with scissors is a bit frightening for children who are used to cutting on drawn lines. It doesn't take long to discover what fun it is. Allow two sessions to complete the project. Begin by having students choose four colors (no more) from the paper on the supply table—they should take **two pieces** of each chosen color. When they go back for more, they should stick with the same four colors.

**Demonstration: [Preface: always cut shapes in multiples of two.]** Put two pieces of paper together and demonstrate: 1)"drawing with scissors" 2) cutting two papers in half, then stacking and cutting all four pieces at once 3) putting two papers together, **folding** and cutting two **symmetrical** shapes. Encourage experimentation in cutting curves, bumps, wiggles, zigzags, and combinations. Expect to be surprised that some students who hate art will love this.

At the end of this session, students should sign their envelopes and *carefully* put the shapes in them. Collect for safe keeping.

 

## Part II

**Supplies:** envelopes of shapes, scissors, glue, colored papers from Session 1, 12" x 18" construction paper in assorted colors, including black and white

**Demonstration:** Have students gather around a table or on the floor—wherever they can best see what you are doing. Use your own shapes or borrow from a student. Dump the shapes out and experiment with different arrangements, encouraging suggestions from the class. Try the shapes on different background colors to show how the background affects the shapes—maybe making them appear brighter, maybe making them disappear.

**New Rule:** If necessary, a fifth color may be added. It's also okay to cut more of a shape (from the first session) to finish out a pattern or make a border, for instance.

Don't allow any glue until students have had time to play with their shapes, trying different arrangements. Some may prefer to make pictures and others, designs. When a satisfactory plan is in place, each element should carefully be glued down.

Early finishers might like to gather up leftovers from their classmates and create group, poster-sized cutouts.

**Variations:** Cutouts with a theme which complements a unit of study. Suggestions: **science**—ocean life, rain forest flora, fauna (or both together), space travel; **social studies**—city life, farm life, life in (name your country); **events**—circus, rodeo, parade, big game, birthday party

# *Head and Shoulders, Knees and Toes*

Grades K–1

The purpose of this project is to get children to pay attention to the human figure, its parts, and how they fit together.

**Supplies:** crayons, 12" x 18" white drawing paper, flannel board, flannel cutouts of head, shoulders, knees and toes, eyes, ears, mouth, nose

**Motivation:** Have the class stand in a circle. Introduce the song "Head and Shoulders, Knees and Toes." Chances are, many of the children will already know it. Sing it once through, demonstrating the motions, then ask the class to join in. Sing it several times, speeding up the tempo with each repetition. Expect lots of laughter! Have the children take their seats.

**Script:** (to go along with the flannel board demonstration) Think about the song we just sang and **raise your hand** if you can name the **first** body part we sang about. [When the answer "head" is given, stick the head to the flannel board. Continue in this vein until all the parts are named in order and placed on the flannel board. Students may need prompting to get the parts in the right order, which is okay, because that gives more kids a chance to answer. You can see them mentally going through the words in their heads.] **THERE! It's a perfect person!** (Laughter!) Oh, it **isn't?** [You can count on somebody naming a part that's missing.] Oh, of course! Raise your hand if you can name something else that's missing. [After all the missing parts are named, continue.] Today we're going to draw people who have not **just** head and shoulders, knees and toes but bodies, arms and legs, hands and feet, necks, hair. Whatever person you decide to draw, think about what kind of clothes the person might wear. [Get some ideas from the class about a person they might draw—athlete, super hero, family member, fireman, ballerina, etc.]

# Head and Shoulders, Knees and Toes*

Head and shoulders, knees and toes, knees and toes,
Head and shoulders, knees and toes, knees and toes,
And eyes and ears and mouth and nose,
Head and shoulders, knees and toes, knees and toes

*Sung to the tune of "There Is a Tavern in the Town"

**Demonstration:** Show students how to start with the head near the top of the page. Have them hunch their shoulders up to their chins to illustrate how important the neck is. Add the neck. The body shape (torso) is sort of rectangular. Ask students where their arms and legs are attached to their bodies. Encourage them to fill the space by making the head and body big enough to end up with the feet close to the bottom. Sometimes it helps to mention that bigger drawings show up better on the bulletin board or in the hallway. As students work, remind them to think about the kinds of clothes different people wear. A second session may be needed to finish the drawings.

**Suggestions:** Modify the lesson to go with units on community helpers, storybook characters, seasons (dressing for the weather).

 

# Self-Portraits

Grades 3–5

Around third grade, children are ready to take a critical look at their own faces, in terms of proportion and placement of features. A white board demonstration works well in introducing the subject. If you are not secure in your drawing ability, practice may help, or you can use the examples here. Make transparencies so everybody can see clearly (no pun intended). You will need mirrors. Acrylic mirrors are available in art catalogues, but they are pricey. A possible solution is to order some for the whole school and share them. (Speech therapists use mirrors, too.)

**Supplies:** white drawing paper (9" x 12" or 12" x 18") or copier paper; pencil and eraser, mirror, magazine photos of faces—try to find faces that are straight on, in a variety of ethnicities

**Procedure:** Before the supplies come out, go through the demonstration and discussion. In order to hold your students' attention, you need to ham it up—expect laughter!

**Script (as you demonstrate what you're asking the class to do):** What shape is your head? (Oval or egg-shaped) Let's see if this is true. Put your hand on top of your head, spreading your fingers as if you were palming a basketball. Now, keeping your hand in that position, place it under your chin. Doesn't match up, does it? Let's try it in reverse. Cup your hand around your chin, then, holding it that way, place it on top of your head. Charlie Brown's head is round, but yours is an oval. [Draw the oval].

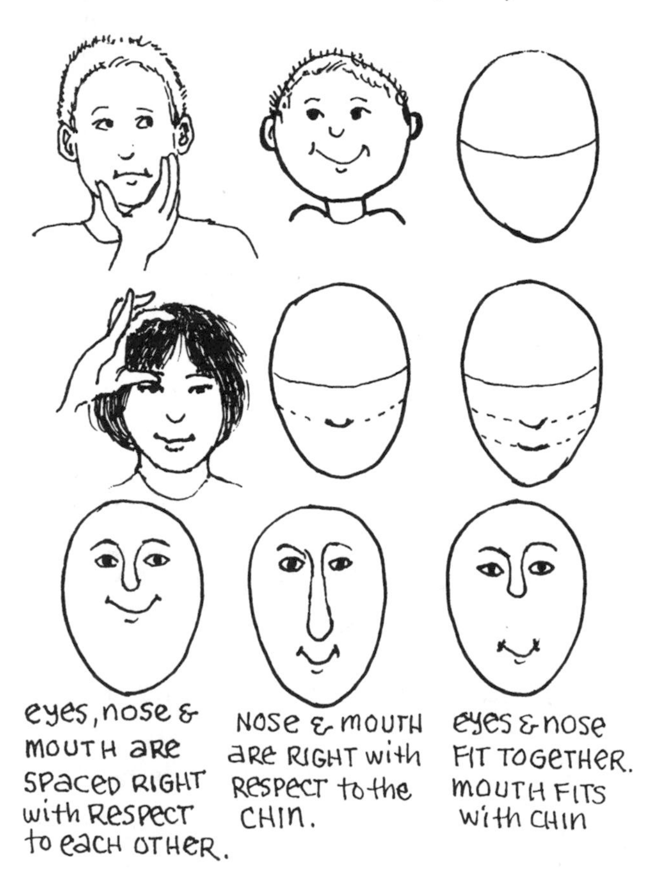

eyes, nose & mouth are spaced right with respect to each other.
Nose & mouth are right with respect to the chin.
eyes & nose fit together. mouth fits with chin

Now put your thumb next to your eye (by your nose) and stretch your middle finger up to the top of your head. Holding that position, put your middle finger by your eye. Where does your thumb end up? On or very close to your chin. What does this tell you about your eyes? It may seem odd that your eyes are in the middle of your head, but you just proved it. [Draw a light guideline on your oval where the eyes should go. Explain that this is common practice for artists. We usually see only finished work, and the little "tricks" have been erased or covered up. The nose ends about halfway between the eyes and chin. The mouth is closer to the nose than chin. Draw in those guidelines, and draw the three funny things that can happen if the eyes are up too high.]

**Back to the script:** Put your index finger on the inside corner of your eye and your thumb on the outside corner. Holding that spacing, move your fingers over, so that your *thumb* is in the corner of your eye. Is your index finger touching the corner of your *other* eye? So how much space is between your eyes? The width of an eye. If you measure across your face in eye widths, you'll find that your face is about five eyes wide. What shape are eyes? [Possible answers might be oval, almond, or football-shaped. Draw the eyes using the guideline, purposely drawing them too far apart. Then, when the laughter subsides, draw them too close together. Now that you've made your point, draw them the proper distance apart, and put a beady, little circle in the middle of each eye. Again, there should be some reaction.] Look at somebody's eyes. What do you notice about the iris, the colored part? Can you see all of it? Open your eyes wide. Can you see all of it now? Your eyelids cover a bit of the iris. You really don't see a whole circle. You can experiment with the iris. [Off to the side of the face draw eyes looking left, right, up, down, and straight ahead. Correct the irises on the face, and add eyebrows.]

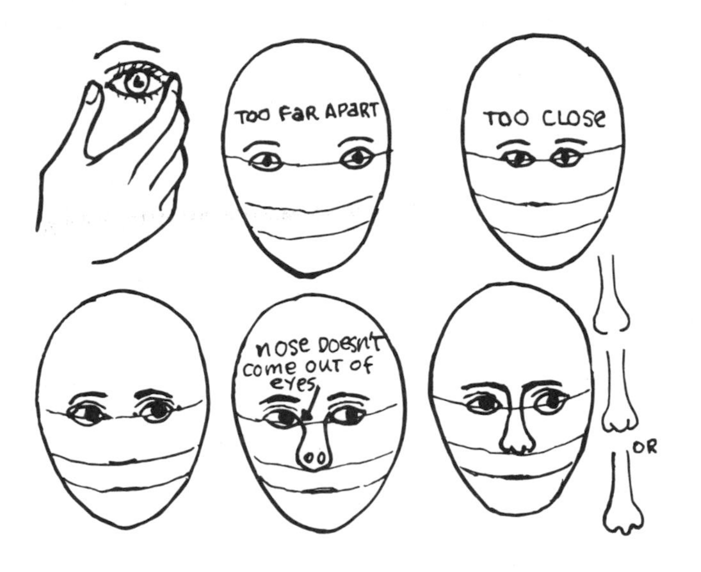


What do you notice about the shape of your nose? [It's narrower at the top and wider at the bottom.] Notice that the top half of your nose is bone—part of the skull. The bottom half is cartilage. Like your ears, it can bend. It's important to understand that your nose is part of the skull when it comes to figuring out where to start drawing it. Why can't it come out next to the eyes? [The eyes are in holes in the skull.] The nose starts close to the eyebrows. [Draw the nose and put two circles near the bottom—loud guffaws.]

We know that noses have holes, or nostrils, but when we look straight at someone's face we only see *part* of the nostrils. To see the entire nostril, you have to tip your head way back. The trick is to draw just part of the openings, noticing that little piece of skin between them. The skin around the nostrils flares out a bit. [Redraw the bottom part of the nose. Here's where photos will help. Students are half-afraid of drawing noses, partly because they can't analyze what they see. Since a photograph is two-dimensional, it's easier to see how and where to draw the lines.]

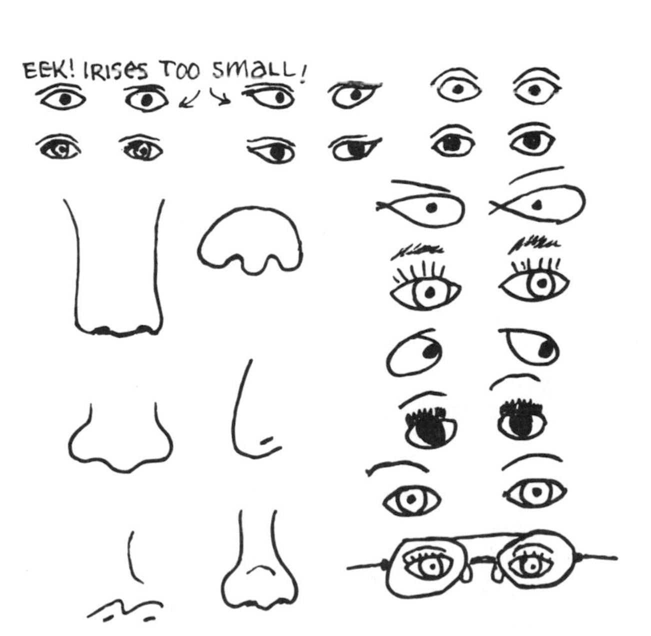


 

Now the mouth. The space between the upper lip and the nose is about half the size of the space between the lower lip and the chin. Starting with your finger at the corner of your mouth, draw an imaginary line straight up to your eye. The corners of your mouth are even with the middle of your eyes. Trace the shape of your upper lip with your finger, noticing the dip in the center that matches up with the skin that hangs down between your nostrils. Notice how your finger goes up and back down as you trace your lip from one side to the other. Now trace your bottom lip. How does it feel different from the top lip? [Draw the lips in the illustration to make the point about "tapering." Also, now is a good time to mention that each person's features are unique in size and shape, but enough the same that we can tell a human face from a dog face. Now it's time to make adjustments. The chin may be too long or short, the face too wide. The sides of the head may need to be brought in a bit, so it doesn't look like a balloon. Explain what you're doing as you work.]

With your finger draw a line from the corner of your eye to your ear. What part of the ear are you touching? Now draw a line from the bottom of your nose around. What part of the ear are you touching? [Make little marks on both sides of the head to indicate position of the ears.] Ears are sort of C-shaped when seen from the side, but if you draw them that way on a front view of the face, they will look too big. You need to flatten them out a bit. [Draw ears sticking out, then close to the head, as seen from the front.]

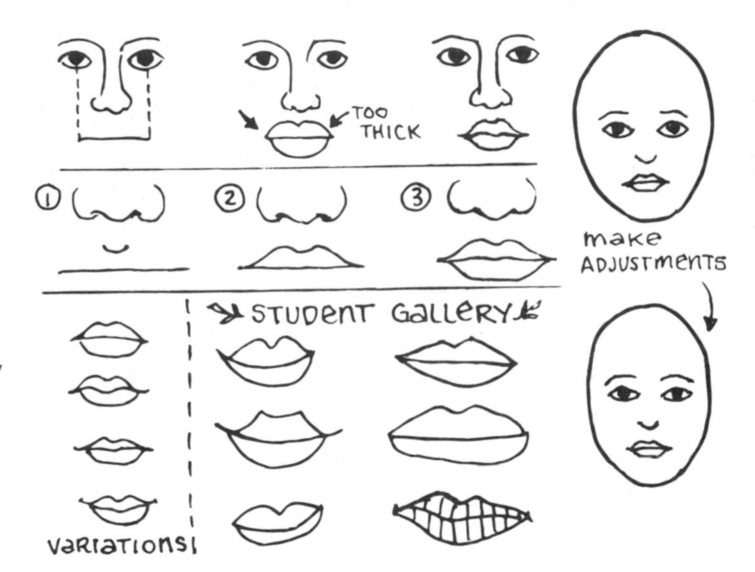


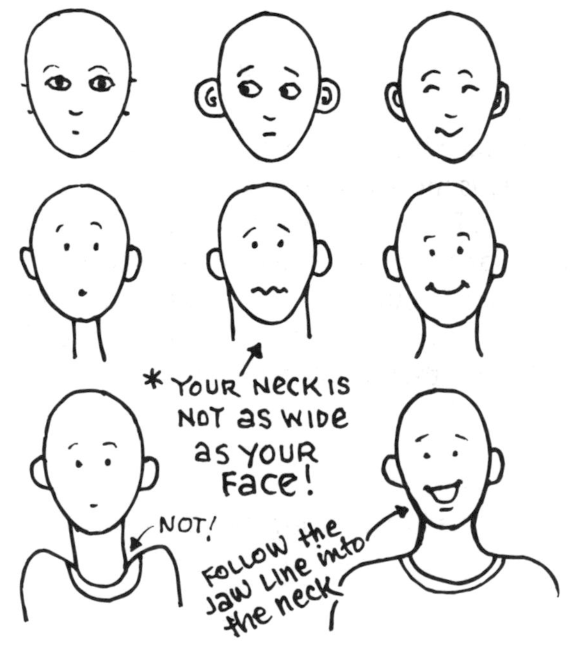


What about necks? There are two ways you can go wrong, the head on a stick Dilly-bar look or the professional football player look. Placing your fingers at your jawline, right below your ears, slowly run them down the sides of your neck and across your shoulders. Feel how the neck gently curves into the shoulders. Turn your head and look at one shoulder, then the other to be aware of how wide they are. Put your hands up to your cheeks, then on either side of your neck. What do you notice? Start drawing the neck at the jawline, and you should come out about right.* [Draw a too-fat neck, then a too-skinny neck, then a neck that curves in from the jawline.]

We're almost done! Hair—is your hair long, short, curly? Where is your hair? Is it *just* on top of your head? What is a *hairline*? You can find your hairline by looking at the distance between your eyebrows and where the hair starts growing. Does your hair grow down to your ears, even if you have a very short hair cut? Look at someone with long hair hanging down. Is there a space between the neck and the hair where daylight shines through? Sometimes it's easier to draw the *shape* of your hair, and sometimes, especially with very short hair, it's better to show the texture.

Your hair doesn't grow **just** on top of your head. Measure up from your eyebrows to find your **hairline**. Follow that line clear down to your ears. If your hair is long, notice how the hair in back is visible next to your neck. Fill hair in the way you comb it. Use curly lines to show curly hair.

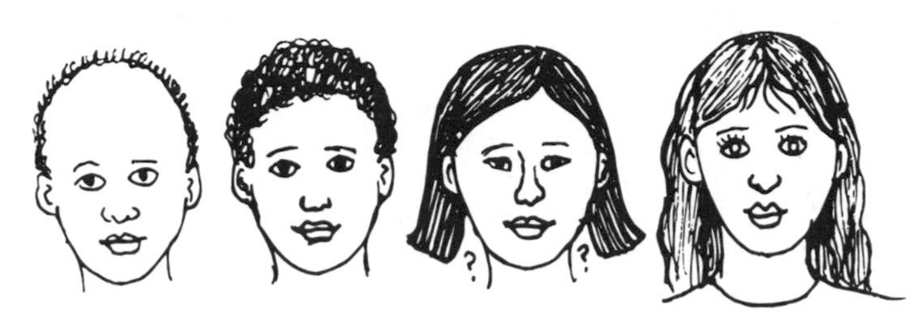

This is a long but pretty entertaining motivation session. Now it's time to pass out the paper and mirrors, which will cause a bit of commotion—as if the kids have never looked at themselves before! Because you have discussed **so much**, go back to the beginning—drawing the oval. This is no easy task for many students (especially third-graders). Since it's a technical problem that may slow them down to the point of not being able to get to the fun stuff, go ahead and help them get that shape or let them use a pattern. Encourage them to try it themselves first. Next, show them again where to lightly draw the guidelines. As they draw, circulate and give verbal cues and reminders. Try to allow enough time for everybody to get a good start, and have another session to finish the portraits.

**READ THIS:** This exercise helps children learn not only how to draw a face but also how artists work out problems to get to the finished product. To some extent artistic ability is more *knowing how to see clearly* than anything else. Demonstration lessons tend to give generic results. To combat this, repeatedly remind your students that every face is unique. Facial features, although similar, are different for each person. **Use that mirror!** It's normal to experience frustration when you're drawing such a precious subject. Try to respond honestly to the work. You may see how fixing some little problem could make a big difference. Go ahead and offer suggestions. When students are frustrated, the last thing they want to hear is, "Oh, that's fine! Don't worry about it."

**Period Portrait:** Tie in with social studies by having students draw themselves wearing head gear and clothing from another culture or time period.

**Artists to Look At:** Van Gogh, Renoir, Mary Cassatt (mothers and children), Rembrandt, Chuck Close, Alice Neel, Leonardo da Vinci, Andy Warhol, Frida Kahlo

 

# Gesture Drawing

Grades 3–5

Knowing how to draw a person is one thing; making it live and move is another. People pictures have a tendency to look stiff. Gesture drawing produces figures in action and lends itself to dance and sports themes—basketball, baseball, football and soccer games, martial arts contests, Olympic sports, ballet, and gymnastics.

**Supplies:** 12" x 18" white drawing or light gray or pink construction paper, yellow chalkboard chalk, cleared table for a model stand; for demonstration—paper placed where everyone can see

**Brainstorm:** Ask kids to name athletic activities they like to watch or participate in, and list them on the board.

**Motivation/ Demonstration:** Explain that the purpose of gesture drawing is to **capture action or movement**. It looks like controlled scribbling. Ask for a volunteer to hop up on the table and go through the motions of shooting a basket two or three times, the last time freezing the gesture just before the ball leaves the hands. Quickly—we're talking seconds—scribble torso, head and neck, arms, legs and feet. (Practice ahead of time!) Have someone else go through the motions of whatever you choose, again freezing at a moment when arms, legs, and body are most engaged. And again demonstrate the technique. Avoid a heavy buildup of chalk.

**Script:** What is the purpose of gesture drawing? [To capture movement or action] Should you worry about the model's face? [No] What about hair and clothes? [No] These drawings are just the beginning. We will get a page full of them, which we will later turn into pictures. Use a circular motion and scribble **lightly**. When you see an arm crossing in front of the body, scribble it over the body. The circular motion, as opposed to up-and-down or sideways, produces the best results. We will take turns posing for each other and begin with forty-five-second poses, then get down to twenty or thirty seconds. The poses will look slightly different depending on where you are sitting. As in the demonstration, each model should go through the entire action once or twice, then freeze. I'll be the time-keeper. Who would like to pose? [There may be a bit of embarrassment at first. If students are slow to volunteer, you might call on someone who you know likes to skateboard or who takes dance lessons. Circulate and see if everyone is getting the idea. Students should not pay attention only to the arms and legs, but also the tilt of the head and torso. If you find someone who's having trouble, do a quick demonstration right there at the table or desk.]

# Gesture Drawing Projects

The artist LeRoy Neiman is famous for his paintings of sports figures and events. To see his work, visit his web page *(www.leroyneiman.com)*. He is definitely an artist to whom kids can relate.

**Big Game, Dance Recital, Track Meet, Skateboard Competition, etc.**

**Supplies:** gesture drawings, yellow chalkboard chalk, crayons, oil crayons, or construction paper crayons, 9″ x 12" and 12" x 18" construction paper in a variety of light colors, scissors, and glue; *Sports Illustrated Magazines*, books on the Olympics (both summer and winter), books on individual sports in which your students may be interested—choose lower grade-level books, and big coffee table books, which are illustrated with color photographs. If you want to tie in with a seasonal sport or activity, choose books accordingly.

**Motivation/ Demonstration: Script:** When we did the gesture drawings, we tried to capture the movement of the figure. That was an important first step, but the drawings don't look like real people. Last time we worked quickly. Today we'll slow down, do some research, and make human beings out of the scribbles. First find photographs in the books and magazines on the table to see how uniforms and costumes look; then color the clothing right on the figures you drew. Since each of you will now be thinking about a particular sport or activity, you might need some poses that aren't on your paper. Get a classmate to pose for you, and quickly get the gesture with chalk like we did last time.* [Looking at a photograph of an athlete in uniform, use one of your gesture drawings to demonstrate how to draw clothes over the chalk, adding facial features, hat, shoes, gloves (feet and hands)—whatever the outfit needs. Keep faces simple—it's the action you're after.

*Some poses, like gymnastic tricks on a balance beam, can't be easily modeled. In those cases start with gesture drawings, using photographs in place of live models.

 

**Background:** When students have finished the figures, they should cut them out, and depending on the size and number of figures, choose a small or large piece of construction paper to use for the background. Format is a consideration—would horizontal or vertical look better? The background is the place to show off the figures. Keep it simple—yard lines, lights, and goal posts; basketball net and scoreboard; bleachers, a multicolored mass; stage, curtains, lights.

Lightly sketch in the background, then color, letting the color of the paper dominate. Arrange the figures on the background and carefully glue them in place.

**Alternative Approach**

Out of all the original gesture drawings, **choose one** to enlarge on white drawing paper (9" x 12", 12" square, 12" x 18", or circle).

**Step 1**—Enlarge the figure as you redraw it in chalk. Think ahead about placement—the figure could be in the center but it doesn't have to be.
**Step 2**—Use **oil crayons** to color the figure—in costume or uniform.
**Step 3**—Choose a color to make a thick outline all the way around the figure.
**Step 4**—Continue to outline the figure using only 3–4 colors over and over, until the paper is full, **OR** after outlining several times, choose two to three new colors to design a shape around the outlined figure, and continue coloring until the paper is full.

**Extension:** Ask students to write poems or short essays about their pictures. What do games mean to them as players? As fans? Why do they enjoy performing? Have them think about the feelings that come with great success and how they deal with mistakes and defeat, on or off the field.

# Clowns

Grades 1–3

**Part I**

**Supplies:** 12" x 18" or 12" x 24" white drawing paper, pencils, erasers, black crayons

**Motivation:** On the board write CLOWN FACE, CLOWN COSTUME, CLOWNS HOLD. The class will brainstorm ideas about each of these categories. A brainstorm is like a rainstorm where **ideas** rather than water pour out. **This is not the time to tell stories about clowns.** Start with CLOWN FACE. Whether they've seen clowns in person or in pictures, ask children to name features that make a clown's face different from our own. List their ideas as fast as you can, asking "anything else?" When there are no more responses, move on to CLOWN COSTUME, suggesting that they think of **all kinds** of costumes—for clowns who are sad, happy, silly, rodeo clowns, clowns who appear at special events like birthday parties and store openings. This list will be long. Encourage more ideas with comments like: "We have named baggy pants—can you think of other things that go along with that?" Mention patterns—what kinds of patterns have you seen on clowns? Polka dots, checks, stripes, zig-zags? Finally, ask what clowns might have in their hands, writing these ideas under CLOWNS HOLD.

**Demonstration:** The purpose of this demonstration is to get your students to focus on the clown. The paper must be vertical, and the clown must fill the paper. (This is not about drawing a circus.) Following the illustrations below, draw on the white board. It's helpful for the kids to see mistakes and how to avoid or correct them. Your initial objective is to help them fill the space, as they are deciding what kind of clown to draw. We think of clowns being happy or silly, but there are clowns like the great Emmett Kelly who move slowly and wear a sad expression. It also helps to mention that people go to clown school to learn how to be clowns. One of their assignments before graduation is to come up with original costumes and makeup. No two clowns look exactly alike.

When the pencil drawing is finished, borrow one student's paper and demonstrate how to draw over the lines with a black crayon. The crayon must be applied heavily, which is difficult for younger children, but it's important for the success of Part II.

 

# *Clowns*

Part II

**Supplies:** clown drawings, pencils and black crayons (for finishing the drawing), watercolors, water containers—half-gallon ice-cream size for groups, smaller for individuals; paper towels; desk or table covers optional

**Motivation/ Demonstration: Before class trace one student's clown for the demonstration.** Gather the class around an easel (or the white board) where you have hung the sample clown. Reemphasize the importance of applying the black crayon heavily. **Script:** Have you ever been eating mashed potatoes and gravy and had the potatoes spring a leak? What happens to the gravy? Yes, it leaks out all over your peas and salad. Think of the black crayon as mashed potatoes. A black crayon doesn't **look** like mashed potatoes, but like mashed potatoes it keeps *what* from leaking out? Right! Your watercolors. I know it's not easy to push hard to get that wax wall around your clown, but you'll see that it's worth it when you start to paint.

[Before you demonstrate, read the section on watercolor techniques and practice enough to avoid any unwanted surprises.]

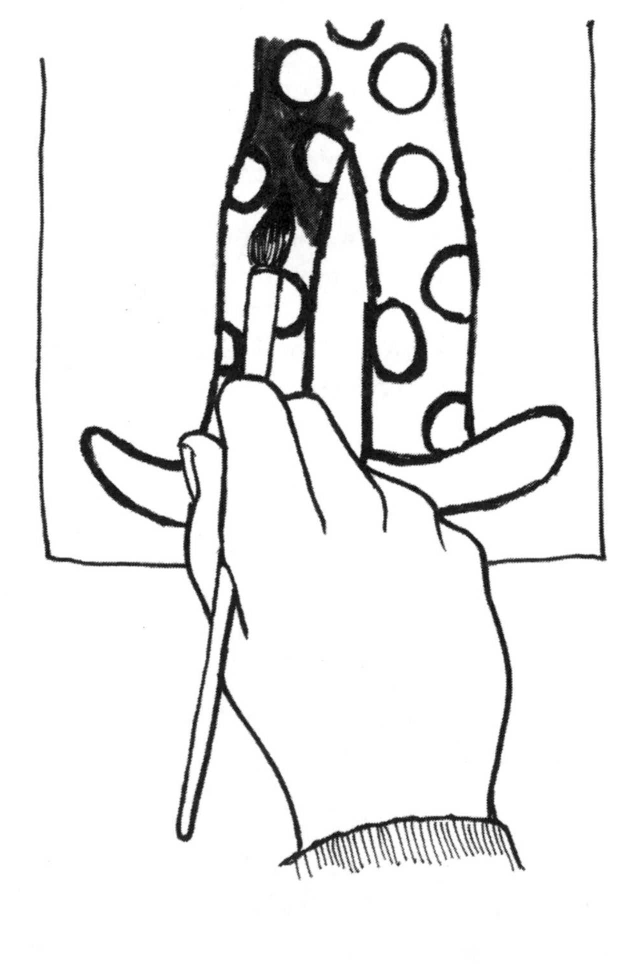

**Demonstrate: How to** make a color lighter by adding water or blotting, and **how to** make a color stronger by loading the brush, using just enough water to let the color spread without making it runny. [This is where the black crayon helps; and remember that a paper towel or a squeezed brush will suck up wet paint.]

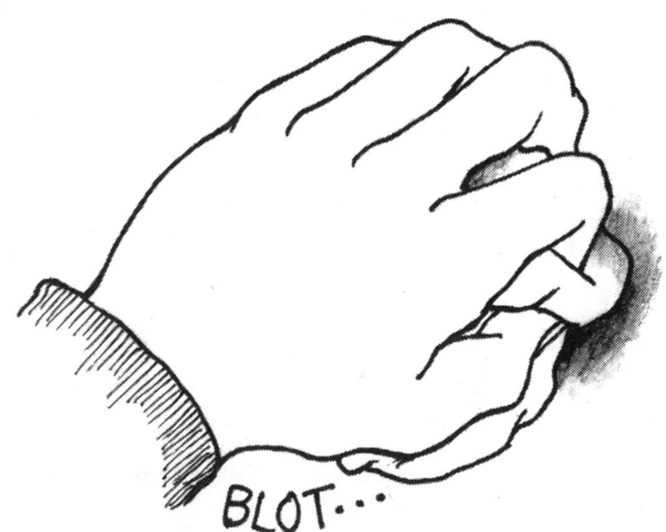

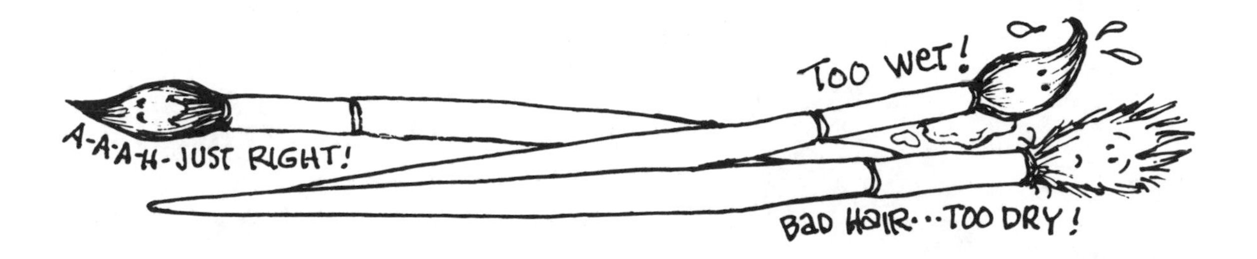
TOO WET!
A-A-A-H-JUST RIGHT!
BAD HAIR...TOO DRY!

**Show** what a too-dry brush looks like—**bad hair**. The water makes the paint "go." **Show** what happens when you paint next to wet paint. (Again, the crayon helps, but not always. Lower elementary children can become skillful watercolorists with practice. Watercolors are a "loose" medium. Part of their appeal is that you can't always tell how the colors will mingle and blend. Younger children aren't as bothered by the unpredictability of the medium as the older ones are. By fourth or fifth grade they're into realism and control.)

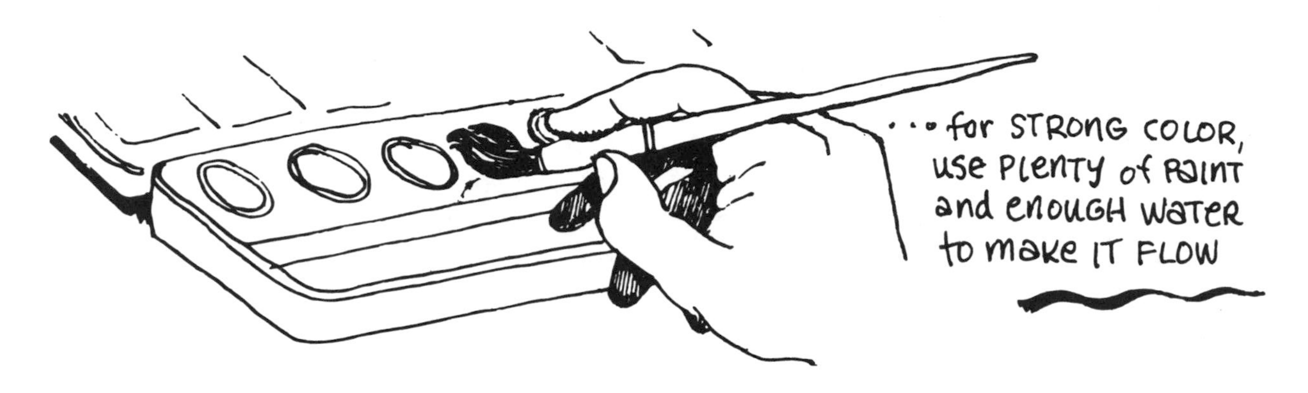
...for STRONG COLOR,
use PLENTY of PAINT
and ENOUGH WATER
to make IT FLOW

**Script:** Since watercolors run together if you paint wet next to wet, should you spend a lot of time waiting for things to dry? How could you keep on painting and still avoid the problem? For instance do you really **need** to paint the whole face at once? What could you do? Yes, skip around. While you're waiting for one part to dry, paint something that's not close to the wet spot. **Talk about color. Script:** Does your clown have a happy face or a sad face? Is the costume ruffly or baggy and loose? Think about using colors that will help show something of your clown's personality. What colors do you think go with happy? [The **warm, sunny** ones—orange, peach, pink, red, yellow—or **bright** turquoise blues and yellow-greens] What about sad colors? Maybe soft blues and violets, red-violets, blue-greens, grays, and browns] After the whole-group demonstration and the students have gotten a good start on their paintings, perhaps they might be allowed to work individually at a watercolor center at specified times. Plan to have another class demonstration when most of the clowns are finished. This will be to introduce the wet-on-wet technique, which makes soft background color(s).

**Background Demonstration:** Use the clown from the last demonstration. (It doesn't necessarily have to be finished, but students shouldn't proceed to the background until the clowns are painted.) If possible, borrow some bigger watercolor brushes from the art teacher. **Script:** Your clowns have gotten personalities as you've finished painting them. Today I'm going to show you a watercolor technique for making soft, delicate colors to surround the clowns. Artists call this space the "background." Background colors will give your clown a nice place to live. The background may be just one color or more than one. What's the most important part of your painting, the clown or the background? The clown, of course! The background helps show off the clown. When people look at your picture, you want them to notice the clown first, not the background. **Demonstrate** the wet-on-wet technique (see page 14): using a larger brush—or your hand if no larger brushes are available—to spread clean water all around the clown on about half of the background area. Using a fairly wet brush, dip into the paint and brush over the wet paper. Rinse. Dip into a second color and let it overlap the first a bit as you brush it on and see how the colors mingle. The idea is to paint with loose, free strokes. Continue to wet (and rewet the paper if it dries) before you paint. Background painting shouldn't take very long. Paint just enough for students to get the idea, then let them try. Don't expect everybody to get it. Some really nice clowns are bound to get buried in the background—it's a learning experience.

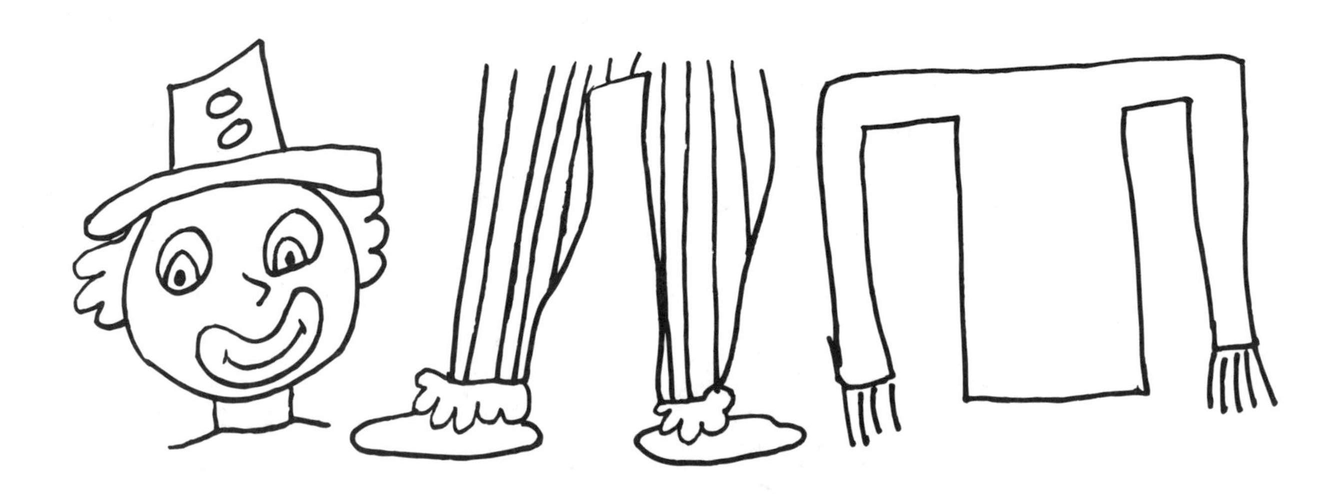

**Follow up:** Write about the clowns. Display paintings and stories.

# Flannel Boards

How and Why

The flannel boards I remember growing up with in the 50s and 60s came with little line-drawn figures in faded colors (or hand colored with crayons by you). The characters were backed with felt so they would stick to the flannel board. Every lower elementary classroom had one, and they were a Sunday School staple for the telling of Bible stories. Using the flannel board was limited to arranging and rearranging the various elements. The most fun you had was perhaps standing one of the characters on its head on the barn roof. Today flannel board sets are brighter and are available in a greater variety of theme sets. Go to *thefeltsource.com* and follow this path: Early Learning>Other Educational Felt Sets>Colors and Shapes. This set includes a large selection of shapes, which in addition to the obvious uses in math and shape identification, can be manipulated endlessly to create art! The hands-on aspect of the flannel board is important in the mouse-clicking world in which we live. I have found the flannel board useful for demonstrations like the Fun With Shapes and Head and Shoulders, Knees, and Toes projects (pages 81 and 90). It also works as a center activity.

You can save money by making the flannel board and felt shapes yourself.

**Supplies:** 18″ x 24" particle board (or something similar into which you can staple); depending on how stretchy the fabric is, felt or flannel* 3" to 4" bigger than the board; staple gun

**Procedure:** Center the board on the fabric. Beginning on one of the long sides, bring the fabric around to the back, and staple in the middle. Repeat on the opposite side, pulling snugly; then do the same on the two short ends. Go back to the starting place, and staple a couple of inches from the first staple (on either side). Repeat all around. When you get to the corners, flatten and tuck the leftover fabric to the back and staple a couple of times. It doesn't have to be pretty.

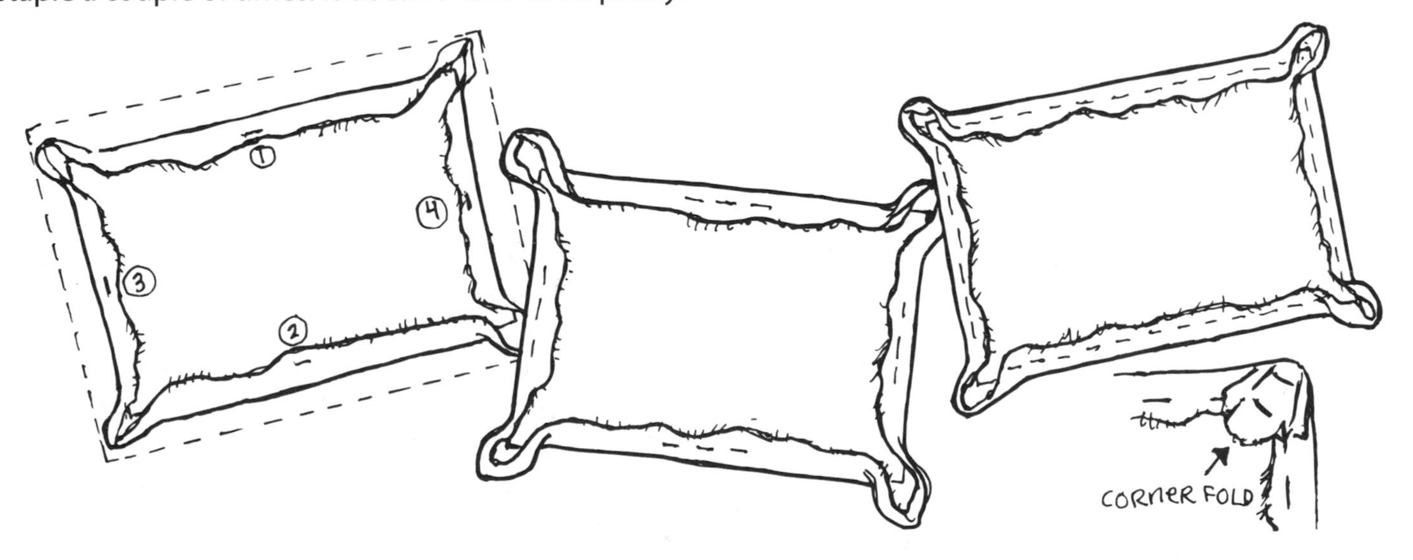


**Shapes:** Cut circles, squares, triangles, and rectangles in several bright colors and sizes. Store shapes in clear plastic sandwich containers. Make other shapes as you need them for demonstrations and themes (natural vs. man-made shapes, for instance).

*Bright colors show up better on a dark, even black background.

 

# Bulletin Board Ideas

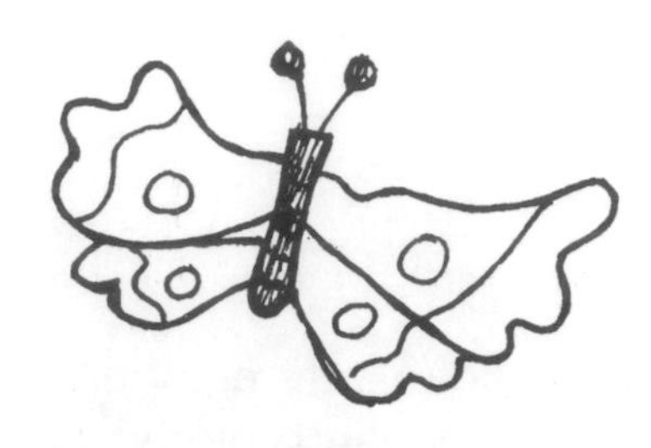

STUDENT SNOWFLAKES ON A BLACK BACKGROUND with PHOTOCOPIES of BENTLEY'S SNOW CRYSTALS MIXED IN....

Think creatively when planning bulletin boards. Rather than purchasing commercial images, think about using your students' artwork. Confer with the art teacher if you have one. Find out what kinds of projects are in process or coming up. You may be able to coordinate to reinforce classroom work with art, and vice-versa. When it applies, put examples of artists' work (reproductions or photocopies) alongside student work—as shown above—SNOW. **Two benefits:** 1) Student bulletin boards are fun and attractive. 2) Displaying the art in this way affirms students' efforts and gives their work legitimacy. (See pages 78, 80, and 81.)

# Bibliography

*Robert Davidson, Eagle of the Dawn,* Ed. by Ian M. Thom, Univ. of Washington Press, Seattle, 1993
*American Indian Design & Decoration*, Leroy H. Appleton, Dover Publications, Inc., 1971
*The American Indians, Keepers of the Totem,* Time Life Books, Time Life, Inc., 1993

*Snow Crystals,* Wilson A. Bentley, McGraw-Hill Book Co., Inc., 1931; Dover Publications, Inc., 1962
*The Little Book of Snowflakes,* Kenneth Libbrecht, Voyageur Press, 2004

*Silhouettes, A Pictorial Archive of Varied Illustrations*, Edited by Carol Belanger Grafton, Dover Publications, Inc., 1979

*Henri Matisse: Jazz,* by Henri Matisse, Pegasus Library, Prestel, 2001 (available on amazon. com)

*Victorian Architecture of Iowa,* (2nd Edition),Wm. Plymat Jr., Palladian Publishing Co., 1997
*Architecture in Education,* Foundation for Architecture, Philadelphia, Ed. Marcy Abhau, 1986
*Hopper's Places,* Gail Levin, Alfred A. Knopf, 1985 (houses Edward Hopper painted)

*A Weekend with Rousseau,* Gilles Plazy, Rizzoli, N.Y. (plants and animals/ jungle)
*The World of M.C. Escher,* by M.C. Escher, ed. by J. L. Locher, Harry N. Abrams, 1979 (animals)
*Butterflies and Moths of the World,* Alain Eid and Michel Viard, Chartwell Book, div. of Book Sales, Inc., 1997
Albrecht Dürer—animals, nature
Aborigine, Mexican, and African folk art (animals)

*Norman Rockwell Illustrator,* by Christopher Finch, Courage Books, 2000;
*Grant Wood An American Master Revealed,* writings by Grant Wood and others, 1995, Davenport Art Gallery, Davenport, IA (landscapes, figures, portraits)
*Mary Cassatt,* Nancy Mowll Matthews, Harry N. Abrams, Inc. in association with The National Museum of American Art, Smithsonian Institution, 1987 (women and children)

*Grandma Moses,* Otto Kallir, Harry N. Abrams, 1973 (landscape, history)

*Medieval Castles,* Conrad Cairns, Cambridge University Press, 1987
*The Book of Beasts,* Edited by E.B. White, Dover Books, 1984
*Knights in Armor,* Shirley Glubok, Harper and Row, 1969

# Children's Books and Illustrators

**ANIMALS**

*Animal Shapes,* by Brian Wildsmith, Oxford University Press
*A Peaceable Kingdom, The Shaker Abecedarius,* Alice and Martin Provensen, Viking Press, 1978
*Animalia,* by Graeme Base, Harry N. Abrams, Inc., 1986
*Color Farm,* Lois Ehlert, J. B. Lippincott, 1989 (also good for SHAPES)
*Color Zoo,* Lois Ehlert, J. B. Lippincott, 1990 (also good for SHAPES)
*Moon Rope,* Lois Ehlert, Harcourt Brace Jovanovich, 1992
*Mouse Paint,* Ellen Stoll Walsh, Harcourt, Brace and Company, 1989
*Hop Jump,* Ellen Stoll Walsh, Harcourt, Brace and Company, 1993
*Pips Magic,* Ellen Stoll Walsh, Harcourt, Brace and Company, 1994
*I Know an Old Lady Who Swallowed A Fly,* Glen Rounds, Holiday House, 1990
*Cowboy,* Glen Rounds, Holiday House, 1991 (also good for figures)
*I Am a Duck,* Linda Bygrave, illus. by Louise Boce, Chrysalis Education, 2003 (part of a series)
*Tuesday,* David Wiesner, Clarion Books, 1991 (frogs)

**ARCHITECTURE/ HISTORY**

*Cathedral,* by David Macaulay, Houghton Mifflin Company, 1973
*Castle,* by David Macaulay, Houghton Mifflin Company, 1977 (**video** *Castle)*
*Castle,* Christopher Gravett, Eyewitness Books, 1994
*Architects Make Zigzags, Looking at Architecture from A to Z,* drawings by Roxie Munro, text by Diane Maddex, Preservation Press
*The Man Who Walked Between the Towers,* Mordicai Gerstein, Roaring Book Press, 2003, (Caldecott Medal)
*Anno's Journey,* Mitsumasa Anno, William Collin Publishers, Inc., 1977
*Anno's Italy,* Mitsumasa Anno, William Collin Publishers, Inc., 1978
*Anno's U. S. A.,* Mitsumasa Anno, Philomel Books, 1983
*This Is the House That Jack Built,* Simms Taback, G.P. Putnam's Sons, 2002 (also ANIMALS)

**FACES**

*Parts,* Tedd Arnold, Dial Books for Young Readers, 1993 (cartoons)
*Green Wilma,* Tedd Arnold, Dial Books for Young Readers, 1993 (cartoons)
*Chuck Close, Up Close,* Jan Greenberg and Sandra Jordan, DK Publishing, Inc., 1998 (inspiring life story)

**FIGURES (People)**

*Degas and the Little Dancer,* Laurence Anholt, Barron's Educational Series, Inc., 1996
*Li'l Sis and Uncle Willie,* A Story Based on the Life and Paintings of William H. Johnson, by Gwen Everett, National Museum of American Art, Smithsonian Institution, Washington, D.C., Rizzoli, New York, 1991